SAUL: THE FIRST KING OF ISRAEL

Saul:
The First King
of Israel

Joseph Augustus Miller

CountedFaithful

SAUL: THE FIRST KING OF ISRAEL
First published in 1853
This edition © Counted Faithful, 2017

COUNTED FAITHFUL
2 Drakewood Road
London SW16 5DT

Website: http://www.countedfaithful.org

ISBN
Book: 978-1-78872-027-4
ePub: 978-1-78872-028-1
Kindle: 978-1-78872-029-8

Contents

Preface

I SHALL not regret that the following chapters have been committed to the press, if, by the blessing of God, they should, even in a single instance, become instrumental in producing a conviction that there is no real necessity for looking to novels, romances, and plays, in order to discover what is stirring in incident, exciting in action, or interesting in the opportunity of studying human nature under a variety of forms and aspects.

To hear some persons talk upon these points, it might be supposed that the Bible had not, in its whole contents, a single page of historic matter – that it did not present a single incident on which a thoughtful mind could moralise – and that there was an utter destitution of material for that study of human nature which is so essential to the satisfactory formation of character. Such persons, therefore, profess themselves to be under the necessity of seeking in other volumes that which they affirm that the Bible does not supply. How far their representations are founded in truth may be ascertained by a careful and candid examination of the structure of the Book. The diligent student of the sacred volume will feel himself in a position to prove that for everything which is ordinarily adduced as giving attractiveness to books for which the Bible is forsaken, there may be found corresponding features of interest in the Book of inspiration. For in its descriptions and narratives the machinery of life looks as unmanageable and incomprehensible, and its processes are wrought out as variously and as marvellously as the most devoted reader of romance could desire. Here, certainly not less than in volumes of another kind, the smooth is most strangely interwoven with the rough – the alteration is made quite suddenly from the low to the high – the reverse of fortune quickly exchanges the bright for the gloomy – and the schemes of men so unexpectedly disappoint all previous plotting and contriving, that the strongest emotions of the reader's heart are brought into activity. Over these pages the mind may be as much fascinated by the succession of incidents which excite, and by the quiet onward flow of existence which lulls and tranquillises, as in the delineations drawn on pages of a lighter tendency. There is this advantage, too, in regard to the Bible, that in the perusal of its touching and often startling narratives, we are saved from the intrusion of the thought, "But, after all, it is not true," – a remembrance which is sometimes very awkward and unwelcome, in the midst of the excited emotions which the extravagance of some work of mere fiction has called up. Over how many portions of the Scripture history must an impartial judge pronounce that "truth is stranger than fiction!" Of all books, too, which were ever written, none meets the student of human nature – the enquirer who is anxious to know what man is, and what he can be – what he can do – what he is intended for – how he can come up to his Maker's purposes concerning him, or how he may fail in this great object – what dangers threaten him – what facilities are afforded him – no book will meet the enquirer proposing such questions for personal and practical purposes with so much promise as the Bible. Its illustrations of human nature are so numerous and so varied, drawn from so many sources, and exhibiting man under such diversity of circumstances, that to attempt the formation of personal character without a perpetual reference to its pages, would be to act as unwise and absurd a part as that man would act, who, pretending to desire proficiency in any branch of science, should content himself with merely reading some lighter books, in which the subject was professedly "made easy," and should never trouble himself to study, nor scarcely to look into, the *standard works* in that particular department.

I have selected the history of Saul as a Scripture study, because I believe that it will furnish ample confirmation of the views which have just been stated. Especially will it be found useful to the young, as a study of character. In comparison with other Scripture memoirs, little has been written upon this piece of biography; and I felt, therefore, that it afforded an open field for observation and prayerful research.

Preface

I look up to the God of the Bible, and laying at His feet this effort to illustrate a portion of His Word, I humbly beg, and ardently long for, His blessing.

James Augustus Miller
1853

Chapter 1
A King Desired

"Nevertheless the people refused to obey the voice of Samuel; and they said, Nay; but we will have a king over us; that we also may be like all the nations; and that our king may judge us, and go out before us, and fight our battles." (*1 Samuel 8:19, 20*)

THESE words afford an appropriate introduction to the narrative of the life and reign of Saul, the first king of Israel. They embody the circumstances under which the sacred writer presents him to our notice. On many grounds the history of Saul should fix itself upon the attentive gaze of the student of Scripture. The son of Kish stands before us as the type of a new order of things in the administration of public affairs among the people of the covenant. He was the first of Israel's kingly rulers; he was elected under circumstances of the most exciting character; yet did he not retain the kingdom in his family, but made way for David and the long line which succeeded him as their father and their head. But chiefly on moral grounds his life and history will repay a careful study.

Its interest is peculiar. It is not the interest of long-continued excellence commanding our satisfaction, nor of high-toned piety appealing to our reverence and exciting our gratification; there is nothing of this, but precisely the opposite of it all. If we were asked what is the prevailing feeling which the study of this history is calculated to produce, we should answer in one word – *Disappointment*. It presents a thoroughly disappointing character. We have the opportunity of looking at it in no abbreviated form; of contemplating it in a great variety of circumstances; of contrasting that which was outward in conduct with subsequently revealed and ascertained motive; and when to the full we have availed ourselves of this opportunity, we cannot describe our emotions in any other expression than that of the most painful disappointment.

Should such a statement as this have at first a tendency rather to repel us from the theme than to invite us to it, yet on reflection it will be felt that this peculiar feature of the history furnishes a strong reason for serious scrutiny and for cautious examination; and this for the sake of our spiritual health, that we may ascertain the cause of a long and painful series of failures of which the life of Saul is made up. As in regard to our bodily health, it is promoted, not so much by the study of the frame in a state of soundness, as by careful investigation when it has come under the influence of disease; so in reference to our moral and spiritual health, to have the heart right with God, and to keep it right, is an end greatly promoted by watching how and where the hearts of others have come under a wrong influence. And he, who is willing to do this – willing carefully and extensively to dissect character – to anatomise conduct – to watch the connection between the external and the internal, and to discriminate between the two – cannot but be thankful for the opportunity which is given him of doing it all, by the preservation in the Scripture records of a remarkably full and complete memoir of the first king of Israel.

To the circumstances, however, under which Saul became king rather than to himself our attention must first be directed. These form a proper introduction to the whole case; and more – they have much to do with the knowledge of our own hearts, and they supply abundant material for thought and prayer.

Taking advantage of Samuel's age and of his sons' misconduct – for it is clear that though the wish was professedly founded upon those circumstances, they furnished no more than the ostensible reason for the course which was adopted – the elders of Israel assembled, and coming to Samuel said, "Now make us a king to judge us like all the nations." We wonder not that such a request was painful to the venerable prophet, and that his burdened spirit found relief at that moment in turning from the ingratitude and waywardness of man to the tenderness and compassion of God, and in casting all its care upon Him, who alone is able effectually to sustain the sinking, suffering heart. How touching is the brief sentence which in the sacred narrative describes his act – "And Samuel prayed unto the Lord!" And he was comforted by that "God who comforteth those who are cast down." The answer of Jehovah might with truth be called a reply of condolence – "And the Lord said unto Samuel, Hearken unto the voice of the people in all that they say unto thee: for they have not rejected thee, but they have rejected me, that I should not reign over them. According to all the works which they have done since the day that I brought them up out of Egypt even unto this day, wherewith they have forsaken me, and served other gods, so do they also unto thee." Then followed the command that Samuel should explain to the people the manner in which they were deceiving themselves in the supposition that it would be better with them when they should have an earthly king than it had been heretofore. Nothing in truth was kept back from them which was calculated to impress them with a sense of their folly, and to lead them to a better mind. But all was in vain; "the people refused to obey the voice of Samuel; and they said, Nay; but we will have a king over us." "And the Lord said to Samuel, Hearken unto their voice, and make them a king."

Now, it is worthy of remark, that in a later portion of Scripture we find allusion made to this very incident, in tones of rebuke and of admonition; we find the Most High commenting upon it, and affording us the opportunity of forming an acquaintance with the views which He held concerning it, and the principles upon which He acted in connection with it. By the mouth of the prophet *Hosea* He sent this message – "O Israel, thou hast destroyed thyself; but in me is thine help. I will be thy king: where is any other that may save thee in all thy cities? and thy judges of whom thou saidst, Give me a king and princes? *I gave thee a king in mine anger,* and took him away in my wrath." (*Hosea 13:9-11*). To a fact, then, which God thus marked out for particular notice in a later period, it cannot but be deemed important that we should give heed. It is eminently suggestive, and from among many topics of instruction which it contains, we may select the following:

I. The request of the Israelites brings before us a melancholy view of the *progress of degeneracy in a community.* Looking at their history from the time of their entrance upon the actual possession of the land of Canaan, though now and then there breaks out to view a hopeful glimpse with regard to their moral and spiritual condition, yet on the whole the scene presented is that of successive generations rising up to depart further and further from God; and now we have the dismal consummation in their effort to destroy, as far as they were concerned, that peculiar and interesting link between themselves and God which existed in the fact – that besides being to them, as He is to all His creatures, their supreme Ruler, He condescended to act as such in a direct and immediate form – standing actually, and to all intents and purposes, in the same relation to them as that which an earthly sovereign sustains towards his subjects. It requires no effort to perceive in this desire of the Israelites the renewed manifestation of the discontented and rebellious disposition which prevailed in the camp at the Red Sea, and on subsequent occasions in the wilderness; but now it was marked by a greater fixedness of criminal resolve and of God-dishonouring purpose. It was the sin of the fathers living over again, but with greater intensity, in the persons of the children. This view of the case is, in a high degree, admonitory. None of us, perhaps, think enough of the connection between ourselves and the future; and yet when we do give our minds seriously to the matter, there is much that may well fill us with awe and solemnity. Among other reasons for the peculiar character of that plan which God has adopted in His holy Word for our instruction – even the method of teaching us out of the history of one people presented to us through successive ages, in the various forms of responsibility arising out of their peculiar relation to Himself – among many reasons for the adoption of such a plan this may be one, the maintenance before our minds of this one idea, that *each age exerts a very considerable influence on that which succeeds it,* and that the men of any particular age are responsible to God in a very large and affecting measure for the characteristics of the period which may come after them.

It is not difficult to bring this matter home to our own feelings. Would it not be an embittering prospect, if as we, the people of the present day, looked forward to the next generation, we were compelled from what now meets our view to entertain the fear that there would not only not be an improvement upon the present condition of men in a moral point of view, but rather a great deterioration – nothing better, but much that would be worse? Do our hearts never bleed at what we feel to be the defective morality of the times? and would they not bleed more if we could only anticipate years rolling on and yet marked by increasing degeneracy? Is not this, in some respects, the threatening prospect before us? Shall we not, by the help of God, labour to prevent its realisation? And is it asked, "How can I prevent it?" – By remembering that the degeneracy of communities is after all the degeneracy of individuals; and that he who makes the effort to prevent in the conduct of a *single individual* the continuance of sin – who attempts in the case of a *single individual* to raise the tone of morals, does so far provide a better state of things for the age that shall come after him. If looking at the clamorous assembly which the narrative brings before us as now surrounding Samuel and asking a change in the form of government, we enquire whence learnt they those low thoughts of God which led them so much to dishonour Him as to wish to put Him aside in order to make room for an earthly ruler? the only proper and correct reply would be, "From those who went before them." We cannot recognise in that crowd the immediate descendants of a race of God-fearing fathers and of God-honouring mothers – the children of those who had sat at the feet of pious Levites and of active and devoted priests. And going further back – how came there to be this absence of a race of God-fearing fathers and God-honouring mothers? How? but because *their* fathers and *their* mothers before them had declined from the ways of God, and had forsaken his laws. The tide of degeneracy had set in strongly after the death of Joshua, and it continued its onward flow until it reached the point of impiety here presented. We live for a future age, and virtually we have the character of that age in our hands, whether as it concerns the nation, the church, or the family. Parents, this subject belongs to you; Christian professors, it defines your responsibility. In regard to the religious instruction of the rising generation, it presents the true standpoint from which such a work should be contemplated, and from which its importance is best discerned as a hopeful provision against the prospect of degeneracy.

II. The scene brought before us by this demand of Israel for a king, teaches us the *perilousness of allowing our thoughts to run in an improper direction, and our wishes to centre upon a wrong object.* And this for a reason, which is very distinctly conveyed to us in the tenor of the narrative – *the absorbing effect of one wrong thought,* and its consequent power to throw into oblivion all those counteracting thoughts and objects which from any other source might be suggested. When the mind becomes thus centred and fixed, it is almost an impossibility to move it, to divert it. Trace the progress of this one wrong desire in Israel, of having a king. Was there nothing to be said on the other side? Rather we might ask, Is it not exceedingly easy to conceive of the counteracting effect which at the first stage might have been presented to such a wish by *a recollection of their actual privileges at the moment?* There is a matchless sublimity – the sublimity of condescension and graciousness – about the very idea of a *theocracy.* But if its sublimity did not appeal to their moral sense, its peculiar advantageousness might have appealed to their self-regard. No other form of government could be compared with it for beneficial results to its subjects. For consider what it involved – the equal accessibleness of the Sovereign to all his subjects – the certainty of having the best counsel under all circumstances – the largest resources both of power and skill at their command – the impossibility of wrong motives affecting the Sovereign's acts – the freedom from the ordinary burdens of government when He was king who could say, "Every beast of the forest is mine, and the cattle on a thousand hills. If I were hungry I would not tell thee: for the world is mine and the fulness thereof." Set, then, we say, against such an administration the form of sovereignty which the Israelites desired. But they did not stay to think thus – nor did they admit another recollection which might well have offered the strongest counteraction to their one wrong desire – even that of *the faithfulness and the loving-kindness with which God as their King had ever treated them.* And so the God-dishonouring wish grew stronger and stronger.

At least, however, it might have been expected that they would be moved by a vivid delineation of the unwelcome consequences which God declared would attend the new arrangement. The prophet was instructed to tell them plainly the things which they must expect to suffer; and though the catalogue included pains and penalties enough to induce them to see that they would pay very dearly for the object of their desire, this did not move them; no! not the assurance that a period of oppression would come upon them, in which they would be unable to consider, not simply their houses and lands, but even their children, as their own. Judge, then, of the power with which their one wrong thought occupied their souls – the victory which it had acquired over their very nature, when for it every other consideration was set aside, and was not allowed to exert any influence at all.

Yet, after all, this is but a picture of real life, applicable to every age. It contains a faithful warning. It says – *"Beware of the first wrong desire,* give it no encouragement. Beware of the first misdirection of thought. Be sure you are right *at first* in your plans and purposes, because afterwards, by reason of the very force with which wrong thoughts indulged exclude all suggestions to the contrary, it may be too late to alter." To the young it especially says – "In the purposes you cherish, the plans you propose, the changes you contemplate, the objects on which you allow your affections to rest, *beware of a mistake at the first.* Religion, comfort, honour, happiness, how often have they all been powerless as motives to reclaim when once the heart has been bent on a wrong purpose, and amid bitter regrets at the last, the soul, undeceived by experience, has mourned, but mourned too late, that it had slighted that lesson of admonition so forcibly suggested by this passage in the history of Israel.

III. It is of importance that we should carefully study *the essential evil of the motive* which here operated in the minds of the Hebrew nation. That motive was – *that they might be like other people.* "We will have a king over us, that we also may be *like all the nations."* They saw other nations with kings, leading them out to battle, and they contrasted the pomp of regal splendour with their own simplicity, and the imposing effect of kingly magnificence with the perfect absence of anything approaching to it in their own case; and they thought – but it was a foolish thought – that they suffered by the contrast; forgetting all the while that that which gave them real honour and essential dignity was, that *they were unlike other nations.* And if in a thoughtful mood we take a survey of the causes which have worked to produce moral desolation in communities from that day until the present, there will appear none whose operation has proved more widely mischievous, more intensely active for harm than this – *a desire to be like others.* In those dreary fields of slaughter where the victims which meet our eyes are souls and their best interests, families and their peace and welfare, individuals and their honour and reputation, we shall find that no murderous foe has cast down so many and left them slain, as this – the wish to be as others are, in those respects in regard to which it is clear that the will of God does not give its sanction to the desired resemblance. Gaze on that form stretched on the dying bed, listen to that cry, "There is no hope!" – that cry repeated often as an attempt is made to tell of One who is mighty to save – "I know it all, but I have sinned against light and knowledge; there is no hope for me." That man once made a profession of religion, and he used to pray, and so to speak of God and Christ, as to leave an impression that he had tasted of the heavenly gift; but he did not like the difference between the rules of the Church and the rules of the world. The world was not very strict, nor would he be. The world pursued its pleasures, and why should not he pursue them too? The world thought there was no harm in the revel and the dance, and why should he see any harm in them either? The world neglected family prayer, and he, too, felt it a restriction, and gave it up. The world did not care about a religion of prayer at all, and talked of large and liberal views on religious tenets and practices, and he wished his views to be understood as being large and liberal like theirs; and so, heedless of the restraints of scriptural doctrine and principle, he fairly committed himself to the purpose of being like them; and now, having made shipwreck of faith and of a good conscience, you see his melancholy end.

Or look where the great white throne is set up; mark well that countenance overwhelmed with shame as those tremendous words are uttered – "Depart, I know you not!" With justice has that sentence fallen, for that condemned one was a hearer of the gospel; yes, and he understood it too, and even felt it. Many a time has that young man left the house of God full of conviction, and ready to resolve that, whatever others did, he would serve the Lord. But he turned to take another look at the world, and the thought came along with the look, that much of his worldly interest depended upon the friendship of those around him, and that if he expected them to be his friends, his opinions and his habits must not be opposed to theirs. He gave in to the principle of being like them;

and, having resembled them in time, his lot now throughout eternity resembles theirs too.

Alas! the wreck of souls which this principle involves! and, we must add, the wreck of earthly comfort, too. Why is that house dismantled and desolate which we have so often passed, with the thought that there was found all that heart could wish? Why? – because, though the position of its occupants was good, it was not quite equal to that of some of their neighbours; and aiming *at being like others,* they exceeded the limits of their income, and were ruined. Why in the gloom of yonder cell do you see that pale, dejected face – careworn and prematurely furrowed? You do not recognise the youth who used to pass you with a buoyant step and a happy smile. Why is he there, and why so changed? Why? Because his companion's dress was of a finer texture, and his purse contained more money, and he could spend it more freely, and the youth thought it was manly to be like his companion, though only dishonesty could help him to the resemblance; and the jail is the melancholy consequence. And why is she an outcast from society whom once you saw in the Sunday School and in the sanctuary, and who, when first she entered upon the duties of her calling, looked so respectable, and promised so well? Why? Because she was not satisfied with her station, because she thought of other adorning besides that of a meek and quiet spirit, because she wished *to be like others;* and, in the vain hope, listened to temptation's voice.

Yes, it is even so. We have here before us one of the chief besetting sins of society in the present day, pervading it in its length and breadth, and leading to consequences of fearful import in time and in eternity – dissatisfaction on the part of individuals with what God has appointed, and a desire for that which, withheld from them by the Great Disposer, falls to the lot of others. It is, though under other forms, the sin of Israel acted over again. Shun it! it is fighting against God. Shun it! it is forgetting that real happiness can only be derived from God's blessing, and that this can only be enjoyed in the circumstances which He in His providence has prescribed for us. Shun it! it is overlooking the fact that, instead of deserving anything at God's hand, we deserve not one of the least of all the blessings which we enjoy.

Our study of this portion of sacred history will not have been in vain if it should lead us to two resolutions:

1. Let God choose our portion for us, and let us be satisfied with His appointment.

2. Let God reign in us and over us by the Holy Spirit. Let us give Him the throne of our heart; He demands and deserves it. And if we feel that this is a duty we have neglected, let us confess our neglect; and, as we implore forgiveness at the throne of the Divine Majesty, let the words of Scripture supply us with a determination, which, carried to that throne in humility, will bring a blessing on our own souls – "O Lord our God, other lords beside thee have had dominion over us; but by thee only will we make mention of thy name."

Chapter 2

Second Thoughts and the Lost Asses

"And the Lord said to Samuel, Hearken unto their voice, and make them a king. And Samuel said unto the men of Israel, Go ye every man unto his city. Now there was a man of Benjamin, whose name was Kish, the son of Abiel, the son of Zeror, the son of Bechorath, the son of Aphiah, a Benjamite, a mighty man of power. And he had a son, whose name was Saul, a choice young man, and a goodly: and there was not among the children of Israel a goodlier person than he: from his shoulders and upward he was higher than any of the people. And the asses of Kish, Saul's father, were lost. And Kish said to Saul his son, Take now one of the servants with thee, and arise, go seek the asses." (*1 Samuel 8:22; 9:1-3*)

IN advancing from the circumstances under which the people of Israel asked for a king, to the actual history of the man in whose elevation their desire was granted, we are reminded at once by the former portion of the passage placed at the head of this chapter, that when God has in His wisdom and mercy withheld anything from us, because He knows it would be no real blessing, because He sees that the feelings which it would gratify are mistaken and mischievous, because in every point of view we should be better without it – when God has done this, and we nevertheless will persist in desiring it, and make up our minds not to be happy without it, He may at length allow us to have our own way; but the very answer to our wishes will come as a proof of His displeasure, and we shall really be receiving a punishment and not an approval. The Lord said, "Hearken unto their voice, and make them a king." "So He gave them up to their own heart's ways." "I gave them a king in mine anger." Far better is it to be made to feel that our desires are wrong, far better is it to have our prayers denied in mercy, to have our wishes disappointed by heavenly wisdom, than to have them granted in divine displeasure. We see this in the case of Israel; let us receive the admonition ourselves. Let our first concern be to scrutinise our desires, to see if they do correspond with God's revealed will; and, if they do not, let us not venture a moment's entertainment of them, lest God should take us at our word, and cause us, in the very possession of that for which it was wrong to ask, to read our sin and folly. In this respect, what thanks we owe to God for denying us many of our most urgent requests, what mercy have we lived to discover in some of our heaviest disappointments; and now, as we review the past, we can lift the voice of praise at the thought of how much kinder a part God has acted towards us in *not giving* what we asked, than if He had hearkened to our voice, and satisfied our importunity.

And yet, though God gave the Israelites their own way, when they would not be convinced of their error, but would covet that which would make them "like other nations," it was not till the very last — not until He had allowed them a further opportunity of reviewing their course. Sometimes arguments which have failed to convince amidst the excitement and warmth of a public assembly, will recur with power and impressiveness in the quietude and retirement of home. Sometimes a course of conduct, which has been determined upon under the influence of misdirected thoughts, will look very differently when it has been thought over in that sober light which solitude and reflection cause to fall on matters brought within their reach. We have felt, many a time, that we could not give our friends a better piece of advice than to *think again* before they acted; and we ourselves, probably, are no strangers to the advantages of acting upon *"second thoughts"* rather than upon first impressions. Thus it is that, when men are going wrong, and are about to bring upon themselves the tokens of the divine displeasure, we often observe that God allows them a little space for "second thoughts" and for maturer consideration. The Israelites accordingly were dismissed to their homes: "Go ye every man unto his city."

In the command that they should retire – in the not proceeding to the actual election of a king at the moment – we seem to hear divine mercy appealing once more to their better feelings, and whispering, "Go and think." "Go and consider your ways." "Ask yourselves once more whether it will indeed be better to set aside God as your sovereign, and to have a king like the other nations?" We discover here the same kindness which had been shown to Pharaoh, when, as the heavy stroke of divine displeasure was about to fall upon that rebel and his land, a time for second thoughts was given him; and, as it is recorded, (*Exodus 9:5*), "The Lord appointed a set time, saying, Tomorrow the Lord shall do this thing in the land." *Tomorrow* – not *today: tomorrow* – by that time he will have bethought himself: *tomorrow* – by that time he can weigh the consequences of further obstinacy: *tomorrow* – and in the meantime I give him space for repentance. The point here singled out for observation is one which often comes before our notice now, if we will carefully watch God's providential dispensations. How frequently does it happen, that when men are bent upon some evil act, some wicked course, which, if followed out, must bring with it the displeasure of Heaven, there occurs an unlooked-for circumstance which delays the execution of their purpose for a few hours or days; which necessitates a pause; which renders it impossible to proceed further just then. They are annoyed at the interruption – mortified at the impediment; but if conscience were awake and faithful, it would hear God saying, "Sinner, I stand between thee and thy ruin a few days longer; I give thee the mercy of a few hours' delay. Go home; go and consider. Go to thy Bible; go to thy closet; go to the mercy-seat: go, before it is too late; and pause before thou dost resolve on persistence in thine unholy desire – in thine ungodly plan." Would that advantage had been taken more often of such a mercy – that the delay had been employed for reflection and repentance! how many a victory might have been gained over temptation – how many a wretched dying bed might have been prevented – how many a soul might have been recovered – how many a broken heart saved! But it has been too often in such cases as it was in Israel's conduct. They did not heed; they did not feel; they did not profit by the voice which said, "Go ye every man unto his city."

We proceed, directed by the course of the passage now under remark, to a new class of incidents, which bring before us the selected

king of Israel, which describe him to us, and which put us in possession of his personal circumstances at the time of being called to the
throne. And, probably, it is but a fair announcement of the general
feeling which arises in the mind of readers of this narrative, when we
say that we can hardly peruse the opening verses of *1 Samuel 9* without experiencing some sensation of surprise at the extreme *homeliness*
of the history, both in its manner and matter. "And the asses of Kish
Saul's father were lost. And Kish said to Saul his son, Take now one
of the servants with thee, and arise, go seek the asses. And he passed
through mount Ephraim, and passed through the land of Shalisha,
but they found them not: then they passed through the land of
Shalim, and there they were not: and he passed through the land
of the Benjamites, but they found them not." Now, the homeliness
of these details may affect us in several ways. It may appear to stand
strangely in contrast with what we know of the more stirring character of subsequent portions of the same narrative. We may deem it
singular, too, that for occurrences in themselves so positively trivial,
so absolutely commonplace, there should have been reserved a place
in the sacred volume. And we may be disposed to think that a more
dignified form of introducing Saul might have been selected – which
greater dignity would have been attained by an entire omission of the
mention of such trifles as Saul's father losing his asses, and sending
his son to seek them.

I. The study of this feature of Saul's history demands that a thought
or two should be expended upon the subject of the introduction into
Scripture of these trivial incidents, these homely occurrences – for
the recollection of every reader of the Bible will immediately suggest
that this is not the only instance in which the same feature meets us
in its manifold narratives. It is not always, indeed, that the impression produced by this aspect of the Scripture record is confined to
mere surprise; it has been allowed to extend further, and many have
professed to find here the grounds of a serious objection against
the claims of the Volume itself to be considered of divine origin.
It has been broadly affirmed, that writers who were under a divine
influence would never have been required to descend to details of so
unimportant a character. We find, however, anything but a source of
discomfort in that which has thus been made a matter of objection.

We affirm, generally, that it is this very circumstantial character of the writings which goes far, in the first instance, to convince us of their being genuine, and having a claim to be received as true. A writer who, merely to answer some private end, makes up a tale, purposely avoids minute incidents. He deals in generalities; because he feels, that if he should descend into particulars, he will but multiply the chances of detection; whereas, a writer who is conscious that he is telling the truth, and only the truth, can afford to state as many minute facts as he pleases; and, indeed, the more of these he is able to introduce the better for his own credibility; because each one, if scrutinised, will only furnish an additional evidence of his veracity. The minutely circumstantial character, therefore, of many of the narratives in the Bible is so far most favourable to our reception of the Scriptures as written under divine influence, that it guarantees their truthfulness – a characteristic, the absence of which would at once constrain us to deny their inspiration.

Still further – it must be acknowledged that matters which, in themselves and separately considered, appear trivial, turn out often, in their connection and consequences, to be most momentous. It is the habit with God to associate the most important results with that which, in its origin, appears most insignificant. To this we shall have presently to return; because the history itself furnishes us with an illustration of the remark. But since God is wont thus to act, it follows that the occurrence of minute detail in Scripture narratives, instead of being opposed to their divine origin, is altogether in favour of it, because altogether in harmony with the ordinary plan of divine procedure.

Nor only so – the purpose of a divine revelation could only be answered consistently with the dictates of the highest wisdom, as the leading features of such a revelation were conformed to the facts and features of our own everyday history. In order to accomplish its professed purpose of being a guide and directory to *man,* it must be a *faithful picture of human life.* Were the aspects under which it presented human life materially different from those under which we ourselves view it, and even participate in it, we should be tempted to say, *This is not the book for us.* Now – considering what human beings really are, and of what elements human affairs are really made up – if from the histories and delineations of the Bible there were a systematic exclusion of all those things which in themselves might be considered as small and unimportant, that Book would fail of being conformed to fact; and we should be taking up ground from which it would be vain to attempt to dislodge us, when we judged that, whoever was the author of the Bible, it certainly could not be the production of a being who had pretensions to infinite wisdom, and that, therefore, it could not have come from God. Great, however, beyond all calculation is the mercy of feeling that the very points which are urged with speciousness and with dogmatism against the claims of the Bible, are the very sources which, when fairly examined, will contribute most to a comfortable conviction of the reality of its divine origin.

II. The incidents connected with Saul's appointment as king were not only trivial, but they possessed in combination with this characteristic another feature – they were of a class to which, in the ordinary way of speaking, we should give the name of *accidental*. And in this respect, the history appears framed so as to teach us the simple but emphatic lesson, that there is a God of providence, and that where, to the human eye, there may appear nothing but an accidental connection between two or more circumstances, there, exists, in the mind of God, the most clearly-intentioned, complete, and beautiful arrangement and harmony. Never was there, surely, a series of occurrences which appeared more purely fortuitous, and which would less give rise to the idea of a premeditated connection between them, than those to which we are now referring. That the asses of Saul's father should have strayed – that Saul should have had so much difficulty in finding them – that they should have taken the direction which they did, bringing Saul so near Samuel – that the idea of consulting the seer should have suggested itself to Saul's servant – all this, does it not appear exactly what we call accidental? *But it was all arranged.* The Lord had appeared to Samuel, and had told him all. And this, if we refer to the close of *1 Samuel 9*, was the very lesson which the good old prophet sought to impress upon Saul, that the hand of the Lord was in the arrangement – that they had not met by chance – but that there had been an invisible hand guiding him, so as to bring him there. It was for this (and how homely is the incident!) that the venerable seer addressed the cook, (*verse 23*), "Bring the portion which

I gave thee, of which I said unto thee, Set it by thee;" and then, that there might be proof how entirely, while Saul had not suspected whither he was going, the mind of the prophet had been prepared for his arrival by that God who leads His creatures in a way which they know not, the servant "took up the shoulder, and that which was upon it, and set it before Saul. And Samuel said, Behold that which is left! set it before thee, and eat: for unto this time hath it been kept *for thee* since I said, I have invited the people." Thus God was in it all. He permitted the loss to occur to Saul's father; He suggested that he should send his son; the animals followed not their own course, but His. He took that servant's mind into His own guidance; the suggestion which came from the servant's lips was, primarily, from a higher source; it seemed a strange coincidence that Samuel and Saul should meet just then – but it was exactly what God had planned. All exhibits a striking view of God as the God of providence, and gives us a beautiful opportunity of seeing Him at work in this department of His operations.

Then our duty is to admit the same truth to its proper place in our own circumstances. As we look back upon our own lives, there stays by us the recollection of many incidents which once appeared not only trivial, but accidental. Their occurrence was the result of no premeditation of ours. They were such as arose seemingly in the ordinary course of events; such as suggested no idea of any special purpose being involved, or such as no human foresight could have prevented. But *why do they stay by us thus?* What is the power which has lodged firmly in our memory things which in themselves seemed to have no claim to so long-enduring a recollection? Why have we not forgotten them long ago? For this good reason: that these very incidents constituted, as we can now see, the springs out of which flowed the most important events in the whole of our history. The path of life, like the course which Saul took when he went after his father's asses, has many turnings; there are a certain number of points at which there is a branching off, and a new direction, given to our footsteps; and this new direction – in how many instances has it arisen out of that which was entirely unpremeditated by ourselves! Had we been left to our own choice – to our own purposes – how differently should we have marked our own way from that which meets our eye, when, in reflective mood, we spread open the map of our own history. In this form, how many of God's richest mercies have been conferred upon us – the tenderest proofs of His watchfulness and compassion. There is one special blessing thus bestowed of which this narrative reminds us – association with the pious and the holy, and the enjoyment of their friendship and their counsels. With what frequency has our introduction to those whom most we are bound to esteem and whose influence over us has been most beneficial, taken place under circumstances which we call accidental? As the disappearance of the property of Saul's father was the first thing which brought him into association with Samuel, so has some equally trivial and seemingly fortuitous circumstance brought us into the society of those who have been our greatest comforters and our most real friends; whose presence with us still gives joy to life, or whose assured arrival at the blissful seats above, is our high encouragement to press onwards, upwards, too. It does not, indeed, require that we should travel far, nor go beyond our own history, to find most undeniable evidence of God at work in providence, and to discover a most precious assurance that He, who in ancient days made His power known and His goodness felt, is *our* God too, working now according to the same principles as of old, and possessing the same claims to love, to thankfulness, and to confidence. Let our gratitude be excited to Him who has been often nearest us and most active for us when we saw Him not – felt Him not; and when our hearts require to be stirred from their lethargy, or roused from their listlessness, let us turn to the annals of our own existence, and reading there our personal indebtedness to the providence of God, let us call upon our souls and all that is within us to bless His holy name.

Such views as those which have now passed before us of a thread of divine arrangement and plan passing through all the varied incidents of our everyday life, should incite to the habitual acknowledgment of God in all our ways. Repeated lessons discover to us our own incompetency to direct our steps rightly amid the puzzling and perplexing paths of life. Is there not, then, a solace valuable beyond calculation in the very idea of a powerful, wise, and holy Being condescending so to associate himself with our movements and to preside over them, as to illustrate the meaning of the promise, and to prove his faithfulness in regard to it, "I will instruct thee and teach thee in the way which thou shalt go: I will guide thee with mine eye"? (*Psalm 32:8*).

And where unforeseen events occur which stagger us, the bearing of which upon our position and duty we cannot at the moment trace, thoughts of the God of providence, "who worketh all things according to the counsel of His own will," and who can see the end from the beginning, should calm every anxiety, and induce us patiently to wait, believing that

> "God is His own interpreter,
> And He will make it plain."

These are the modes in which our present life may be divested of the painful suspense which arises out of its many uncertainties and continual mutations. For notwithstanding that which meets our eye, it is still a fact that *all is arranged.* The chart of the divine purposes is gradually unfolding; but the measure and the manner of that unfolding we must leave in the hands of the great Contriver. And why not? Have we any reason to doubt His providential care – His wisdom and His goodness? What if Scripture itself testified with less clarity on these points – if others' experience gave us less light on the matter than really we discover in both? Still we should have no reason to fear that our welfare was left to accident, or that the advancement of our interest was a mere matter of chance, for *our own personal history,* thus far, is proof to the contrary. We have this evidence, in addition to the other sources of confirmation; and we only use this testimony fairly, as we rise to the enjoyment of our privilege – as we live so as to manifest our full belief in the leading, guiding hand of "Him who is invisible" – as we testify, in our turn, to the unbelieving, God-forgetting world around us:

> "'Tis to us no cause of sorrow,
> That we cannot tell today,
> What it is will come tomorrow,
> 'Tis enough that we can say
> He whom we our Father call,
> Knows the future – knows it all."

III. Another thought suggested by that portion of the narrative now under consideration is this – that since, from God's concealment of the future, we cannot tell what He may intend to do with us and by us, it is our duty to hold ourselves in readiness to undertake any service which He may require us to render, to enter upon any position He may call upon us to fill. When we see Saul taken from the quiet discharge of the common duties of life, and placed upon the throne of Israel, we see the truth set forth – in an extreme case, we admit, but therefore only the more impressively – that it is utterly impossible for us to predict what God may have in store for us. Of all the possible or probable events which might have happened to Saul, that of becoming king would most certainly have been set down by himself and by others as the least likely ever to occur. If such a prospect had been suggested to him on the morning upon which he left his home, in the hope of repairing his father's loss, he would have hardly admitted its possibility. And it would not be difficult for us to fix on positions and duties, respecting which, if a fellow-creature were to intimate even the most distant prospect of their ever forming a part of our personal history, we should have our reply ready at once, that it was as little likely as that we should he called to fill the throne of these realms. Yet these may be actually in store for us.

But how, it may be asked, can we be prepared for that which is as yet entirely concealed from us – that which we cannot even anticipate? To this it may be replied, that there are certain qualifications which are requisite alike for all positions, and which render us, in a good measure, ready for any service. Such, for instance, are diligence and fidelity in meeting the claims of our present condition, whatever it may be. Such is the effort at mental cultivation, by the acquisition of useful knowledge, and by the employment of our thoughts upon the information thus gained. To these we may add, *that habit of working from principle* which will ever be found the best aid to perseverance, because it stands opposed to all fitful excitement. The more self-acquaintance, too, which has been gained – the more dependence upon God – the more prayerfulness, watchfulness, and concern for God's glory – the more real religion, in fact, which a man possesses, the more satisfied will he be in any position, however lowly – the more prepared for service, however exalted. In the pursuit and possession of such qualifications there can be no loss sustained; for if God should bid you go on in the same course of duties to which you have addicted yourself for years, the more pleasant and welcome will be your perseverance in them; and if God should open another door for you – if He should change the nature of your employment, and alter the character of your duties, the discipline and exercise involved in your discharge of the claims of one sphere will issue in your greater fitness for the responsibilities of another.

It is here that we see the positive advantages of that state of mind which induces us to feel that we are the Lord's, and which leads us to consecrate ourselves to Him, under a felt conviction that we are not our own. There is nothing which can, more certainly than this, keep a man satisfied with his present condition, *as assigned by God,* because it teaches him to feel that, in filling it, he is obeying the direction of the Supreme Disposer; and yet the same principle will keep him ready for every fresh call, ready to hear the voice of God asking, "Whom shall I send, and who will go for us?" and to reply, "Here am I, send me."

To the young, especially, the language of friendly admonition might here be addressed, founded upon the vast dissimilarity between what Saul was found doing, and what he was subsequently called to do. You cannot tell what God may have for you to do. Reject no opportunity, therefore, of mental cultivation, and be diligent in the great matter of spiritual training. Improve your minds; take care of the progress of your souls. God can turn all your acquisitions to profit. Besides, to take in the whole case – to contemplate every supposable event – even if on earth God should not see fit to place you where your mental and moral acquirements might appear to turn to fullest account, remember that this is but the threshold of your existence; that there is a world where, in the highest sense, His servants serve Him – serve Him, as well in acquiring larger measures of knowledge and grace, as in putting these forth in appropriate acts of adoration and obedience; and remember, that the larger our attainments are upon earth, the more we have gained of what is elevated in moral characteristic, or high in intellectual acquisition – the more advanced will be the point from which we shall start on our heavenly career, the more we shall be prepared to drink in heaven's streams of light and love, and with new vigour to serve the Lord of heaven in the thousand forms in which, in those blissful seats, we may be called upon to prove our consecration to Himself.

Let these meditations on the striking change in the condition of Saul, and the circumstances under which it took place, conclude with one reflection – a reflection which harmonises with the thoughts which have just been suggested. Saul, in the pursuit of a lesser good, met with the offer and promise of *a crown*. We say he was fortunate. But there is a better fortune which meets us wandering through this desert land, and often in pursuit of objects of inferior worth. An offer of a crown is made us, but it is one of imperishable material:

> "*That prize with peerless glories bright,*
>   *Which shall new lustre boast,*
> *When victors' wreaths and monarchs' gems*
>   *Shall blend in common dust.*"

An offer of a kingdom is made us, but it is of "a kingdom which cannot be moved." Wearying ourselves we may be with that which, if we do find it, if it actually become our own, we cannot always retain; but the message of heavenly love meets us and says, "Wherefore do ye spend your labour for that which satisfieth not?" It is the voice of a prophet which we hear – of "that Prophet," a greater than Samuel. Oh! ye who are seeking the poor, perishing things of time and sense, know ye not that in devoting your time, your energies, in that direction, you are turning aside from the prospect of "an inheritance incorruptible, undefiled, and that fadeth not away" – offered to you by One who makes a larger sacrifice in opening it to you, than Samuel did when he presented Saul with the kingdom? He, indeed, stood aside, and consented to retire into privacy, that Saul might be king; but Jesus stooped lower far that you might have the honour. He humbled Himself, even unto death; endured the cross that you might wear the crown. And lest you should urge, as an excuse for your neglect, the claims of this present life, and tell how they must be provided for, He says, "Seek ye first the kingdom of God and his righteousness, and all these things shall be added unto you." Then turn aside, and accept the offered grace; for, solemn as it is to utter it, yet most certain is the fact, that no hearer of the gospel will ever come to inherit the final and unchanging sentence of God's eternal displeasure – no hearer of the gospel will ever come to spend his eternity in the regions of the lost – who will not also have to carry in his memory, as ages roll along, the overwhelming thought, that while he dwelt in the world which he has left, and wandered along the earth to which he will never return, there was made him, on the part of the Lord of heaven, an offer in good faith of an immortal crown and a glorious kingdom, but that he had not the wisdom to accept them, and now it is too late to seek them. From such a recollection may divine grace preserve us!

Chapter 3

The Choice Young Man
and Goodly

"See ye him whom the Lord hath chosen, that there is none
like him among all the people?" (*1 Samuel 10:24*)

THERE are two forms in which the man who is steering his vessel
over the perilous ocean may ascertain the course which he
should keep, and receive admonition of the dangers which he should
avoid. There may be the well-known lighthouse, reared near the
treacherous rocks, speaking its language of caution, and yet at the
same time affording its tranquillising assurance, that so long as that
caution is followed, there will be safety. And in passing and re-pass-
ing, the mariner may at length become so used to the sight of it,
as that it shall be seen from afar, without any particular emotion,
and certainly without any very exciting dread of the danger which
it serves to indicate. But there is another beacon which the sailor
sometimes discovers, whose warnings are conveyed in a still more
emphatic form. It is not the lighthouse which the hand of science,
directed by kindness, has reared – it is not the buoy that floats over
the treacherous sand; but it is the shattered vessel which has come
too near the point of danger – whose steersman, not perceiving or
not heeding the caution, has allowed it to advance whither it could
not retreat; and now it lies, rent by the dashing billows, a very picture
of desolation –its timbers breaking, its stores floating, its passengers
lost. Such a spectacle, we readily imagine, would be most impressive,
and would serve to render the familiar caution of the ordinary beacon

doubly vivid and valuable: and if the pilot who beheld it had begun to grow careless, this would put him again on his guard; and if he had been at all indulging in a feeling of security, this would remove and destroy it. The spectacle would bring out the reality of the peril, and would lead him to the reality of duty and responsibility.

Now, what these two forms of admonition are to those who "go down upon the deep, and do business in the great waters," the precepts of God's holy Word on the one hand, and its historic warnings on the other, are to those who are voyaging over life's ocean to the haven of eternity. The language of God's precepts is kindly admonitory: these say enough to keep us right; but we are apt to get so used to their teachings, as that they lose their power – used to them, as the sailor is to the beacon on the rock, or to the buoy floating over the sand. We want something more. We want something that shall tell upon our security and heedlessness more vividly, and with more realised impression; and we have it, we find it in the historic warnings of God's Word – *in wrecks* – the wreck of peace – the wreck of character – the wreck of comfort – the wreck of hope – in the cases of those who have trifled with the voice of divine precepts, and have refused the blessings of heavenly direction. Such is the spectacle which is presented to us in the history before us – *it is a wreck,* and one of no ordinarily distressing character.

But among the spectators of a vessel driven on the rocks, and dashed to pieces by the violence of the surge, none would be so much moved as those to whom it might have occurred to see that very bark when it was launched, or when for the first time it left the harbour, as the sun shone brightly, and the sea stirred only in playful ripples, and its own course was so steady and majestic, that all looked auspicious, and it seemed but natural to predict that its path would be safety and its haven peace. To spectators who could recur to past hopes thus excited, the effect of beholding the wreck would be additionally distressing; the contrast between what had been, and what was then before the eye, would be telling in the extreme.

And this enhancement of melancholy interest undoubtedly attaches to our present theme. Nothing could be more auspicious, nothing more attractive, than the commencement of that career which terminates, as we shall see, in a moral wreck; and the lessons which the narrative of Saul, as a whole, is intended to teach, will be felt powerfully in proportion as we study the hopeful circumstances which attach to his outset in life. There were actual manifestations of conduct on his part which looked like promise of the brightest future. We particularise two.

I. The first was his *dutifulness* as a son, and the consequent regard in which his father held him. In these respects, he really stands before the young as an example and a model. The Spirit of God, who has recorded the perversity of Eli's sons, and the unworthiness of Samuel's sons, has brought into notice the immediate and ready obedience of the son of Kish, (*1 Samuel 9:3, 4*). The duty, to which his father called him, when he sent him to look after his lost property, was far from pleasant. His preference, had he consulted mere inclination, would probably have been to stay at home, or to go on some errand of a different character, but *his father wished him to go;* and, with a readiness which indicated a previous habit of filial obedience, he went. Unlike either of the two sons mentioned by our Lord in His parable, the one of whom promised, but did not go, the other of whom refused, but afterwards relented – there was about Saul an unhesitating promptness which is most exemplary. Let it be remembered, too, that this was at an age when his position was no longer that of a mere dependent child. He was grown up; he was old enough to be a king; and he might, therefore, have felt disposed to exercise a will of his own. But, for all this, he does not appear to have ceased to feel rightly as a child; filial obedience must have grown with his growth; for when his father gave the directions to go, he could not have yielded more willingly, and acceded more unhesitatingly, had he been only a child. And where is there the son or the daughter to whose conscience and judgment the example of Saul, in this respect, must not commend itself? You must feel that you would have read it with very different emotions if it had been written that, when his father asked him to go, he had objected and made some excuse; and if you had discerned beneath that excuse the symptoms of any feeling of this kind – that he was now too old to act out the lessons of his childhood, and that it was more manly to say, "No!" to his father than to give that prompt and cheerful, "Yes!" You prefer to see what is very discernible here, that to do anything which could gratify his father, which could relieve his mind, which could mitigate his anxiety, which could promise to restore his property, was to Saul both a duty and a delight. Of all the things which we find written in God's Word in regard to the parental and filial relations (and there is very much written there on these topics), we can discover nothing which would lead us to suppose that *the filial obligation can ever expire.* In childhood it is beautiful as a natural affection, called into exercise in association with natural dependence upon parental kindness and attention; but it is still more lovely and beautiful when it becomes more thoroughly a matter of principle; and when, actual dependence on parental resources being no longer felt, the judgment still demands and dictates the respect and veneration of the child for the father and the mother.

We are not surprised to find, as another part of this interesting history, the *regard which Saul's father entertained for him,* as evinced in the incident, recorded, (*1 Samuel 10:2*), that when Saul and his servant were departed from Samuel, and had reached Rachel's sepulchre, in the border of Benjamin, at Zelzah, two men met them, who having announced that the lost property was found, added (and with what naturalness and simplicity does the addition fall upon our ears), "Lo, thy father hath left the care of the asses, and sorroweth for you, saying, What shall I do for my son?" The loss of his property was considerable; but the loss of his son was a far greater privation – "A wise son maketh a glad father;" and now that the father missed the son who had often made him glad, he could not help exclaiming, in his deep solicitude, "What shall I do?" Saul occupied at home a place of important interest in his parent's view, and now that his place was vacant, the blank was painful. For a son who caused him shame, who had often well-nigh broken his heart, he would indeed have sorrowed, but how differently! This was a mourning over one who was valuable to him; one, to whom if calamity had befallen, it had happened to him, not as a graceless runaway, but while engaged in doing a kind service, and manifesting a genuine obedience to his parent. He was, we repeat, a *valuable* son; and God's goodness to His creatures is eminently seen in this, that He has associated with a right course of action in the social relations of life, *the privilege of being valuable* – a privilege which is not to be sought merely for its own sake, and never for the sake of using it as a ground of merit in the sight of God; but still a privilege which, when viewed with deep and becoming humility, cannot but be gratifying to our best feelings, as a real honour conferred by God – a step in moral elevation for which we are entirely indebted to His goodness. And where, if we can thus acquire a value in the sight of our fellow-creatures, where should we so much desire to be of value as in the estimation of those to whom, more than to all others, we are indebted – who watched over us in our infancy – who have borne the burden and responsibility of our education – whose time, and property, and care, have been expended in the promotion of our comfort – who know us best, and love us most? To them it is impossible that we can be sufficiently grateful; at least, then, let us so act as to acquire and preserve their esteem. It is painful to see children outliving the esteem of their own parents. Their love it may be impossible finally and absolutely to survive; but while natural feelings may yet exist, all personal respect and estimation may be lost: and over the child, whose birth gave joy to the family circle, and lighted up hope in the household, there may come a day when the parent's breaking heart shall utter the cry of distressing anguish, "Would that he had never been born!" Let children remember that though, on natural grounds, they may look for a parent's affection, there is something else to be aimed at, without which that affection will involve no joy, either to those who feel it, or to those who are the objects of it; *that* something is a *parent's genuine esteem*.

We should still, however, be doing injustice to the character of Saul as a son, if we did not specially notice one circumstance, in addition to those to which we have been making reference. We have seen his obedience, and the evident regard in which he was held by his father; but there meets us in this part of the history *a touching thoughtfulness regarding his father's feelings*. For before the men met him who announced that the property was found, we read that Saul had said to the servant who was with him, "Come, and let us return; lest my father leave caring for the asses, and take thought for us," (*1 Samuel 9:5*). There is a beautiful delicacy about this feature in filial character. Aware of the love which his father felt towards him, and of the value in which he held him, he thought more of his father than of himself, and converted that very parental esteem into a fresh reason for regard for his father's feelings. He put that question, which, if it had been more frequently put, would have preserved the comfort of many a family, and prevented many grey hairs from going down in sorrow to the grave – "But *what will my father say?* what will my father feel? what will he think if I do this?" Saul thought of the distress which his protracted absence would cause at home. Bold and determined, he might have said, "Well, I shall go on; I don't like to be defeated when I have undertaken anything; I don't mean to give it up;" and he might have justified his dogged pursuit of the lost property on the plea that he was doing as he was bidden. But no; there was an exquisitely nice balancing between what he knew of his father as a man careful of his possessions, and what he knew of him as a tender parent; and the latter prevailed. He could not bear that a needless distress should overtake him; he could not bear that he should have a moment's anxiety which it was in his power to prevent; and though, to be sure, it would have been very gratifying to himself, as a young man, to have reaped the reward of his perseverance, to have found the animals, and taken them home in triumph, and to have shouted his arrival along his father's fields until the echo brought the old man out to hail his son; yet he would not consent to purchase this gratification at the risk of occasioning his father an hour's unnecessary uneasiness; and he was ready to go home, as the messenger of his own disappointment, and to encounter the awkward sidelong glance by which some of his neighbours and companions would intimate that they were quite aware of his want of success – he did not mind this, if by so doing he could make his parent happy. He deemed it not unbecoming *to make his father's feelings the guide of his conduct.*

We cannot read the varied references which Scripture makes to the parental relationship, and not feel that the test which Saul applied in ascertaining the course of duty is one which God often and urgently demands that we should employ. "The joy of a father," or "the heaviness of a mother," are considerations of vast moment with God; and are, therefore, matters which cannot safely be trifled with by children, even of elder growth. "Will this rob my father of rest; will this add to my mother's sorrows?" – let this be the question before you take your course, and shape your plan and purpose. The answer of your conscience may divert you from some private gratification, and you may be exposed to the laugh of some false friends, for adopting this test and carrying it out manfully; but anything is better, whatever it be – disappointment, mortification, and sneers – anything is better than to stand and look coldly on a parent's grief, and to sting that bosom on which in infancy your head has often rested to catch the smile or even the fond tear of love. A contrast, deep and striking to the conduct of Saul, is found in that scene in the patriarch Jacob's life, in which his ten sons, having, in order to gratify their evil passions, sold his favourite child into captivity, sent home his blood-stained coat, with a false and heartless message; and, rather than reveal the truth, suffered their father to sorrow from day to day, listening without emotion to his moans: "Joseph is without doubt rent in pieces; I will go down to the grave sorrowing." Who would desire to be classed with them? Who would not rather say, "O my soul, come not thou into their secret; unto their assembly, mine honour, be not thou united?"

Long as this feature in Saul's character – his regard for parental feelings – has detained us, it is impossible to render it too prominent a matter for observation. For the sake of society – for the sake of the church – for the sake of the world – it becomes a duty to reiterate the command in these degenerate days – degenerate, in no small measure, on account of a diminished regard to filial duty – "Honour thy father and thy mother."

II. Besides the particular point which we have reviewed, there was in Saul's character a large amount of *right-mindedness* under circumstances which might have proved a strong temptation to manifestations of an opposite kind. Sometimes we see, among our fellow-creatures, great excellences overborne by great and lamentable defects. We hear it said of a young man, "Yes, he is a good son; but when you have said that, you have said all. He is so conceited, so much an upstart, so perverse towards all but his own immediate friends, that you lose many a time the recollection of his excellence in the personal inconvenience which you suffer from the other features of his conduct." No such thoughts as these, however, are suggested by the narrative of Saul.

1. There would appear to have existed, in his case, what might have been a considerable *temptation* to *personal vanity;* and yet, in the earlier portion of the narrative, there cannot be traced the slightest approach to it in his demeanour. His appearance was evidently in his favour; and whether he sat down at the guest-table where Samuel presided, or moved along the high-road, he could not but be noticed, for it is written, (*1 Samuel 9:2*), he was "a choice young

man, and a goodly: and there was not among the children of Israel a goodlier person than he: from his shoulders and upward he was higher than any of the people." Now we are very far from saying that such external endowments are to be thought nothing of; they have their uses: but there is no misapplication of them so entirely beside the mark, so contrary to their Giver's intention, as that which takes place when they become the means of exciting the personal vanity of their possessors. There is no course so entirely against reason as this. In the goodly form, such as was Saul's, we see – we ought to see – the hand of God; to discern His power, to hear Him telling us how goodly a creature man was when first he stood, the masterpiece of creative energy. But beyond this all is humbling; for the finest outward form has within it a depraved heart, and what now strikes the eye as comely, is to become the food of worms – recollections these which should excite to an anxiety for the possession of higher – of spiritual blessings – of a new heart in the present state of existence – and of that consummation of blessedness in which the very body is to share at the last day, when our expected Lord shall come, "who shall change the body of humiliation, that it may be fashioned like unto his own glorious body, according to the working whereby he is able even to subdue all things unto himself." Thus, and only thus, will a goodly appearance cease to be a perilous possession.

To be vain on the ground of personal charms is to act a senseless part, for these imply no merit, and promise no long duration. The winter of age must be contemplated, as well as the spring-tide of youth and the summer of manhood and womanhood. Besides, it is the mind that gives value to the man: and what is the casket if it be empty? However beautiful its exterior, it disappoints if there be no gem within. Let the voice of reason, let the voice of religion prevail against personal vanity. We do not suggest going to the other extreme; there is no merit at all in that extreme disregard to their personal appearance which some affect, and which renders them slatternly and slovenly. Adopt as your rule, "My body is the Lord's" – this will conduct you far enough in your care for it, while on the other hand it will rebuke and repress all that is unworthy or inconsistent.

2. If Saul's appearance did not lift him up, neither does he at first seem to have been rendered vain nor to have been unduly elated

by his new circumstances. There is nothing more difficult to bear than a change from a lower position to one which is several grades above it. There are some beautiful instances, indeed, in which men have stood the trial well, and have carried into an elevated sphere all the humility and simplicity which marked them in the ordinary walks of life. But these are rather the exceptions than the rule. With many a man the very day of his transition to a higher path in outward condition has been the period from which is to be dated his pitiful absurdness – his perfect uselessness – his moral fall. But look at Saul and watch him, at least for a time. The kingdom was proposed to him. Mark his answer, (*1 Samuel 9:21*), "Am not I a Benjamite, of the smallest of the tribes of Israel? and my family the least of all the families of the tribe of Benjamin? wherefore then speakest thou so to me?" And that this was not merely the making of a fair show is proved by the fact, that when subsequently he met his uncle, who was extremely inquisitive as to what might have passed between Samuel and his nephew, he contented himself with saying what transpired between himself and the prophet about the missing animals, but "of the matter of the kingdom he told him not a word." He does not proclaim himself king, but the very reverse. The people are gathered together: he knows why – a king is to be appointed. It would appear only natural that he should have been visible on such an occasion; but when they sought him he could not be found, for he had "hidden himself among the stuff." And even after this, he went quietly home, without affecting the slightest pomp. He had the good sense to wait; and the very next time we see him he is "coming after the herd out of the field." He evidently felt that when he was wanted to act as king he would be sent for, and this was a plain proof of right-mindedness. Thus did all augur well for the future. Such humility and modesty demand our admiration. It was the *first* becoming the *last,* and from the effect which it produces on our mind as we read it, we may learn, in passing, the lesson that there is no elevation superior to that which is held by the man who preserves, amidst the vicissitudes of life, a demeanour uniformly simple and unpretending; and, further, that those greatly err who conceive that in order to be raised in the estimation of others, they must attach a large share of consequence to themselves.

3. He manifested the same right-mindedness in bearing without resentment, conduct which was intended to irritate him, and which was very much calculated to produce that effect. There were then, as there always will be under analogous circumstances, a certain number of individuals who could not bear to see another in a position above themselves; who thought themselves fully as entitled to it as he; and who, because they could not attain to it, nor deprive him of it, set themselves to annoy him in it. "The children of Belial said, How shall this man save us? And they despised him, and brought him no presents," (*1 Samuel 10:27*). And how did Saul act? With what significance the sacred writer adds, "But he held his peace." Now it was much to be so quiet where human nature – as we, perhaps, know from experience – is very apt to be excited. But the secret of this silence is to be found in that characteristic which we have just been considering. If he had attached an overweening importance to himself, you would have seen a very different course of conduct. But it was the absence of this which saved him. The utterances of the men of Belial proceeded on the presumption that at the moment self-importance was the prominent principle at work in Saul's heart; it was a shaft aimed at this, as they imagined that it would not only be there, but uppermost. Mistaken, however, as to the mark, they failed in hitting and wounding. His views of himself and of his position were not, just then, sufficiently high to be touched by the arrow of their malignity. Many are the blessings attendant on humility, and among them this is not the least, that it denies opportunity to those who would seek to wound us through pride. In fact, the question whether or not things which are intended to annoy and irritate us shall succeed in their purpose, depends entirely for its answer on the states of mind which we habitually cherish. These states of feeling may be either as the warrior's complete and well-secured armour, from which the adversary's darts fall back, harmless and blunted; or they may be, for the want of the exercise of right principle, like the defenceless garb, whose very texture not only admits the hostile lance, but helps to hold it.

Saul held his peace, and this course soon silenced his foes. We know, indeed, that it does not always follow that a man is not resentful because he is quiet. There is a silence which as much means, "I will have my revenge," as if those words were uttered in angry tones.

But it was not because Saul was meditating a project by which they would be made to suffer that he was silent. He was not saying within himself, "Now they shall wince for this; they will doubtless be in some trouble soon, and I shall not help them; they will want me to fight their battles for them, but they will find out that they had better not have talked as they did," – and yet he did adopt a plan of making them feel their error. That silence did mean something: it was the reserve of a spirit which was only waiting the first opportunity of convincing enemies of their wrong by doing them a kindness. "They say, Can this man save us? They shall see, for I will do my best to save them, by saving the kingdom." And so he did; for when the Ammonites came up he was prompt at his post, and as successful as he was prompt. But even there the most interesting features in his triumph were his self-control and magnanimity. For when the people said to Samuel, "Who is he that said, Shall Saul reign over us? bring the men, that we may put them to death;" Saul answered in a moment, "There shall not a man be put to death this day; for today the Lord hath wrought salvation in Israel."

Such are the representations afforded by Scripture of the character of Saul at the time at which he was called to the throne. And from all we have said, what might not have been hoped for in regard to the future? Yet our hopes are destined to be disappointed; and if for no other reason the earlier portion of Saul's character should be studied, at least this should be done for one purpose – to teach us that while natural excellences may attract attention and admiration, the permanent manifestation of them can only be secured by that *real religion* to the power of which Saul, alas! eventually proved himself to be a stranger. Without this, no natural goodness can be depended on; and, however great may be its attractiveness, it must ever suggest the dread of itself becoming "as the morning cloud or as the early dew."

The instruction to be derived from this portion of the narrative, widely applicable as it is, especially deserves the notice of those who are young. Be all that Saul was when he set out in life, but secure the same endowments of character from a higher source than mere nature. Seek them from God, as the result of His Spirit's teaching – His Spirit's operation in the heart. Seek them, as the effect of love to Jesus constraining you to imitate His example. Then, having obtained them, seek their permanence and growth from the same source. This will be the great security against that disappointment which arises from such a deterioration of character as a little later we have before us in the history of Saul.

And, especially, let those who profess to mould their characters according to religious principle, take care lest the excellences which attach to the conduct of the unconverted should be wanting in themselves. Let not the filial obedience, the right-mindedness, the humility, the forgiving disposition of the young man who does not profess to be under religious influence, rise up to rebuke the self-sufficiency and inconsiderateness, the want of deference to parents and friends, and the unlovely perverseness of the young man who has made a Christian profession; lest, when the question is asked, "What do ye more than others?" the answer of faithfulness and of fact must be, "Nothing more, and even not so much."

Chapter 4
The First Wrong Step

"Saul reigned one year; and when he had reigned two years over Israel ... Samuel said to Saul, Thou hast done foolishly: thou hast not kept the commandment of the Lord thy God, which he commanded thee." (*1 Samuel 13:1, 13*)

IF for a moment we put ourselves into Saul's position, and endeavour to conceive what our thoughts would have been, had we been suddenly met in our ordinary walk of life with the announcement of a change in circumstances and condition so extraordinary as that which befell him, we can readily imagine that there would be *two* points on which we should desire satisfaction. First of all we should ask, "Am I quite sure that the hand of God is in this matter – that there is no mistake about it? Is it really God's intention that I should give up my present condition, and enter upon another so very different, and to me so entirely unexpected? I should like to be quite sure that I am right before I proceed another step." And our second anxiety would be about our own competency. We should say, "I feel at home in my regular duties; habit has taken off the sensation of burdensomeness and difficulty in connection with them, but this is like beginning life over again. How shall I encounter my new duties, and meet the new claims made upon me?" And these thoughts were, without a doubt, those which actually moved within the bosom of Saul, for they are those for which we discover God making a merciful provision as soon as Samuel had communicated to him the divine intention respecting the kingdom. The prophet gave him proof that the hand of God was in it, by mentioning to him circumstances which would occur on the way home, which no human foresight could have predicted; and the incidents turned out exactly as the servant of God had said that they would. Nor did he leave him with any depressing view of his own incompetency, for he was told that even before he reached home he should become a sharer in special endowments attributable to the Holy Spirit – an inspiration from above by which he would be rendered equal to the duties and difficulties of his station, so that he would become quite "another man;" his mind rising to his circumstances; his thoughts, and views, and feelings corresponding with his new position.

And of this there was given evidence in his "prophesying" – a term which is here not to be taken as referring specially and restrictedly to the foretelling of future events, but which is used in the wider sense of speaking, under immediate inspiration, of things which would not otherwise have occurred to his mind; or in regard to which, if they had come within the range of his thoughts in an ordinary way, he would have expressed himself in a manner far less fervent and impressive, because his conceptions of them would, but for this supernatural agency, have been far less vivid and comprehensive. The narrative represents the prophets whom Saul met as under the influence of a sacred ecstasy, singing the praises of Jehovah. It is quite evident that there was an observable difference between men under ordinary feelings and under this sacred impulse. Bystanders could recognise the agency of the Spirit of God; and an utterance made under this kind of inspiration, although its object might not be to predict future events, was called *prophesying*. They recognised this in Saul, and they said, "Is Saul also among the prophets?" Such an incident would greatly relieve his mind. The inference was clear that God, who could thus, by an act of sovereignty, make him in a moment a sharer with prophets, could qualify him for anything else. All this did not involve, of course, a *permanent inspiration*, but it told that, as on that occasion, and by nothing short of an act of God, Saul had found himself doing what nothing else but God's immediate power could ever enable a man to do, so on any and every future occasion he might be sure that God would raise him above his own personal incompetency, and lead him by a higher wisdom than his own – "the wisdom that cometh from above." No wonder, then, that under these circumstances God said, "Thou shalt be turned into another man," and that it is written, "God gave him *another heart,*" – sentences which are most expressive, however, as suggesting that a man may be a recipient from God of qualifications most valuable, of powers the most important, for the sphere he is called to occupy; that he may, by the act of God, be endowed with talents to fill the most exalted and most responsible positions, so that he shall, in comparison with his own former feelings and previous attainments, be hardly like the same man: and yet – these sentences suggest – that with all these received from God, he may live destitute of other, higher, and sanctified gifts – gifts ready to be bestowed, waiting to be asked for, but the need of which he may never have felt. There may be *"another heart,"* and yet it may not be *"the new heart,"* and *"the right spirit,"* and an individual may be turned into *"another man,"* and yet, in the scriptural sense – in the only sense which brings with it the favour of God now and the prospect of heaven hereafter – he may not have become *"a new man."*

In this, his act of condescending kindness, then, God was saying to Saul, "I mean you to be king; you may rest satisfied that you are in the path of duty; and I show you, by your being thus made at home with these prophets in their peculiar calling, that I can make you at home in that other vocation to which you are equally strange." And by this act God taught the people, too, the lessons which they needed to learn. It was quite as important for them, as it was for Saul himself, to know that he was king by divine appointment. And if, after giving proof of enormous folly in their contempt of theocracy, they still had a grain of common sense left, and were disposed to ask about the competency of the man who should rule over them, their enquiries were met at once – *Saul was among the prophets.* It was strange that he should be among them, and some of them could not help expressing their surprise. Cannot we imagine the countenances of that group, all thunderstruck and inquisitive, which the sacred historian brings before us when he says, "And it came to pass, when all that knew him beforetime saw that, behold, he prophesied among the prophets, then the people said one to another, What is this that is come unto the son of Kish? Is Saul also among the prophets?" And there seems to have been in that group one man more thoughtful than the rest; perhaps a good old man who had lived long enough, and meditated on God enough, to know how that the admission of a thought of the Supreme into a seemingly mysterious matter will wonderfully clear up difficulties, and throw a naturalness into that which men of the world would think immensely marvellous. "And one of the same place answered and said, But who is *their* father?" – a sentence which must be interpreted by the tone and the accent, as though he had said, "But whence did *these* prophets gain their powers? How comes it that *even they* prophesy? There can only be one answer to that question. God is the source of their inspiration. He made them what they are. And He who gave them what they have, can bestow the same endowments on others as well as on them; on Saul, of whom no one ever dreamt as being among them, as on others who appeared more likely to be of their company. Think of the hand of God in this, and then you can make it all out." A good theologian was he, and his theology was all the better because it was so simple; and none the worse because it started out with the doctrine of the divine supremacy and sovereignty, because it referred everything to God, and accorded to Him His right of doing what He will with His own. If we notice, too, it is said that this speaker belonged to "the same place" as the prophets. It would seem as though he had not lived for nothing in the neighbourhood of the prophets; that instead of being ill-natured, jealous, and discontented because God had denied him gifts which He had accorded to them, he had thankfully availed himself of the opportunity which arose out of a residence so near them, and had gained from them all the knowledge that he could; and now he was, as compared with his neighbours, a wise man, ready to solve a problem or clear up a doubt; and in this respect his example is well worthy of imitation.

But Saul was to have one other proof that without hesitation he might, in all the future of his life, seek and find *his all in God*. What is a man without friends, especially if he have great responsibilities pressing around him, and great cares devolving on him. And who are our best friends? Not those who talk about us the most – not those who trumpet our praises, and advertise our talents; but those who think of us in our homes, and who come, knowing we are care-worn, to ask if they can help us, and who stand ready to do us a service which only God's eye can see, a kindness the knowledge of which is confined to our house, and to the chambers of the heart made glad by this personal attention. If ever man wanted such attentions it must have been Saul, when he found himself all at once king over Israel. Possibly at the moment his countenance showed that he did, and there came over him the look which told that deep anxiety had taken possession where hitherto not a furrow had been lodged by a single heavy care. That tall form stooped, and those shoulders fell, as though a material weight and burden had suddenly been fastened on them. And now the election is over – its excitement is past – its bustle subsided. He must go home as well as the rest of the people; but ah! in how different a state of mind from theirs. Men can often bear up in public under circumstances beneath which they break down immediately they are alone. It is hard to refrain before others; but it is impossible by one's self. That man has no bowels who can read without deep emotion how, when Benjamin stood before Joseph, as he sat in his capacity of governor of Egypt, this power of self-control in public was so severely taxed that it had well-nigh given way; and how, as it is written, he "made haste; for his bowels did yearn upon his brother: and he sought where to weep; and he entered into his chamber, and wept there." Men break down, when alone, beneath other pressure than that of fervent love. Duty, responsibility, and felt difficulty will produce the same effect. And real friends know this, and hence they will not say, because they see a man keep up in public, "Ah! he is quite equal to his duties; he will do very well now; we may leave him:" but rather they will, because he has kept up before others, expect that it is all the more probable that he will not be able to do so in private; and they will think of him at home, and they will follow him thither, with their prayers at least; but, if the opportunity serves, with their presence too. Thus they will show that they have *hearts* – hearts, in the worthiest sense of the term – and that their hearts have been indeed "*touched*." All this comes before us in the history. Saul is not allowed to *go home alone*. No! he must be sustained by sympathy and friendship; he shall not feel solitary; he shall not go unattended: "And there went with him a band of men, whose hearts God had touched." But mark that word – *God!* Even these emotions of sympathy – these proofs of attachment – these manifestations of heart – are not, by the historian, allowed to pass before us as just the natural effect of the working of men's own minds under the peculiar circumstances of the case. *God* was in them; *God* excited them; and in the fact that *God* touched their hearts and disposed them favourably, Saul was to gain a new encouragement, a new assurance of being in the path of duty.

This power, too, which God possesses of touching the hearts of men, and moulding them to His purposes, is one which it were well if we more distinctly recognised and more completely confided in. We can clearly see that Saul did not court popularity. Of course, it was most desirable that he should have the affections, the sympathy, and support of his fellow-Israelites. But he did not make a long address to them, and use any vulgar art of ingratiating himself with them. On the other hand, he was far from indifferent; he was anything but careless as to what people thought of him: he seems to have preserved the happy medium, and to have just done this – to have acted so as to deserve their esteem, and then to have left it to God to secure their regard – *to touch their hearts*. Nor did he pursue this course in vain. There were many hearts "touched." Oh! it is better, easier, safer, more dignified to get at men's hearts *through God's power over them,* than to seek their good opinion by any lower efforts; and it is a precious truth, confirmed and illustrated by this case of Saul, that God has this power over the hearts of our fellow-creatures – that it is His prerogative so to influence them as to secure to us, in the prosecution of His service and of duties which are undertaken at His call, that encouragement which makes us cheerful, that co-operation which promises to render us successful.

How favoured, then, was Saul's position as he found himself king! Endowed, as we have seen him, with many natural excellences – with many inviting features of character – he is made the recipient of a most impressive series of divine interpositions, calculated to cheer, encourage, and sustain him. What may we not expect from him in the administration of the kingdom?

"Time works wonders;" so we often speak, and more often think than speak. But when we do say so, we generally have in view some lengthened course, some protracted period, during which the effect produced has been gradually worked out; and we are not startled nor excited by the result. But occasionally, time works wonders very rapidly; and it is the rapidity with which the unexpected result has been brought about – the little time which has sufficed to manifest the striking change – it is this quickness which alarms and appals us. The narrative of Saul presents such a sudden alteration. Without a notice of what is coming, we find him doing that which is visited with painful marks of the divine displeasure. We instinctively exclaim, "But how long has he reigned? It surely must have taken some lengthened period to obliterate, or even to weaken, those good impressions which were made upon him. Recollections, such as he must have cherished, could not have faded very quickly, and good resolutions could not so soon have been positively and recklessly broken through." But ah! these expressive words with which this thirteenth chapter commences, "Saul reigned one year; and when he had reigned two years," – what mean they? but that, during the first year all seemed to go on very well; yet that, ere he had reigned two years, there had commenced a course of declension which prepared him, at the close of the second year, to take his *first wrong step* as a king.

At this first wrong step we are imperatively called to stay and investigate – for it was in his case, as it has been in thousands of others – that the *first* digression from the course of integrity was ruinous – the *first* forsaking of the path of duty was fatal in its consequences. He never recovered himself; and the principles which were set going then are to be detected in active operation throughout the whole of his history, till that day arrived when, on the field of blood, pierced by the arrows of the Philistines, but more keenly wounded by the stings of his own conscience, he fell on his sword, and died.

The nature of the sin itself demands explanation. Turning to *1 Samuel 10:7, 8*, we find Samuel saying to Saul, in prospect of the kingdom, "And let it be, when these signs are come unto thee, that thou do as occasion serve thee; for God is with thee. And thou shalt go down before me to Gilgal; and, behold, I will come down unto thee, to offer burnt-offerings, and to sacrifice sacrifices of peace-offerings: seven days shalt thou tarry, till I come to thee, and show thee what thou shalt do." Now, from the whole tenor of the narrative, we conclude that this direction was not intended to apply to any one single occasion, but that it was to be a general rule for his guidance; that whenever a difficulty arose, whenever an emergency occurred, Saul was to proceed to Gilgal, as a place of religious resort, and to wait there for Samuel's arrival, which, he was given to understand, might not be until seven days had expired. Looking, then, at this requirement, we are at once struck with the abundant wisdom which is manifest in it. It was a simple but a very significant way of telling

Saul that he was not an independent monarch – that he must not act as though he were – that as he was divinely appointed, so he must consent to be divinely guided – and that Samuel was to be the medium through which this guidance was to be obtained. His was a limited monarchy – limited by the right to control which God maintained. This requirement, therefore, was a test by which it might be ascertained whether or not there existed in Saul's bosom an acquiescence in God's plan. In the same way, all divine precepts become tests of character. If they are followed out, they afford the proof of a spirit of obedience; if they are neglected, they expose the lurking spirit of opposition. But to have to wait seven days – this was very galling to a man in Saul's station; not to be able to act without advice, and to wait so long before it came – this was very trying. Of course it would be; that is, if pride had begun to work, if any deteriorating influence had begun to operate. Of course it would be, if he had grown impatient, and independent, and self-sufficient – but *not otherwise.* If his heart were still submissive, the more his patience was taxed, the greater the proof that, in submission, he preferred God's will to his own – nothing could be more calculated to bring out the certainty that his heart was really right with God than such a requirement, which made him stand before his people as a patient attendant on divine teaching, unwilling to stir till the prophet had visited him. On the other hand, if he could not brook restraint, then he would be sure to take objection to this rule which God had laid down. Such a view of the case gives a clarity to the whole recital, and removes all idea of mere arbitrariness from the arrangement.

And now the time of emergency had come – the Philistines were up in arms – the public danger was great. Saul is found at Gilgal – Samuel does not arrive – Saul is impatient; at length, according to his own calculation, the seven days are expired. Not a moment longer will he wait – not another half-hour will he allow the prophet. It may be that he has begun his reckoning from the wrong point, and it would be better to err on the safe side, and wait a very little longer, rather than infringe upon the divine command. Did such a thought arise within him? He would not brook it. He did not mind running the risk of offending God: and be sure, that when even the possibility of doing wrong can be lightly viewed – when, there being a doubt even, we take advantage of that doubt to gratify our own passions, rather than act on the principle of denying ourselves in case we should be wrong – be sure, that when we do this, our hearts have begun to be callous, the searing process on our conscience has already commenced. And then, as it often happens in such cases, Saul had scarcely committed himself to the wrong course before he was detected. "Bring hither," said he "a burnt-offering to me, and peace-offerings. And he offered the burnt-offering. And it came to pass, that as soon as he had made an end of offering the burnt-of-fering" (and before he had presented the peace-offering), "behold, Samuel came." (*1 Samuel 13:9, 10*).

It is clear that his conscience told him that he was wrong, from the vain excuses which he made. He told Samuel that he did it reluc-tantly – "I forced myself." He charges Samuel with delay and want of punctuality – "Thou camest not within the days appointed." He assigned a religious motive – "I had not made my supplications to the Lord." And here we see that sort of special pleading which always shows a consciousness of guilt, and which, at the same time, always exhibits an aspect of contradictoriness. If it really was so, that Samuel was in the wrong, and he in the right, where was there any need of apologising? If he was right, why should he have had any reluctance at all to offer those burnt-offerings, as he says he did hes-itate – "I forced myself." If the real reason was that he had not made his supplications, and that he could not delay this act any longer, ought he to have waited so long? ought he to have even waited at all? All this showed him to be in the wrong. He stood convicted of impatience which could brook no delay; of pride which could not endure to stand second – no, not even where God stood first; of disobedience, which set its own determination against God's will, and chose to follow it out.

This was Saul's first offence against the arrangement which God had made. But God saw fit to visit it with punishment. It was for this the prophet said, "Thou hast done foolishly: thou hast not kept the commandment of the Lord thy God, which he commanded thee: for now would the Lord have established thy kingdom upon Israel for ever. But now thy kingdom shall not continue." (*1 Samuel 13:13, 14*).

Alas! that this *first wrong step* should have proved so fatal to the prospects of Saul. Is it objected that the penalty was severe, for not waiting a little longer than he did, till Samuel arrived? We answer,

"Shall not the Judge of all the earth do right?" And though we should never volunteer a justification of the divine proceedings as though they needed this, yet we may find that there is a power in such thoughts as the following, to throw light on the divine dealings in this case.

1. Sin is not estimated by God according to its outward form, but according to the amount and extent of the principle of evil embodied in that form. There may be as much of downright rebellion against God in what men would call a little sin, as in a series of what they would describe as flagrant offences. And when we say of a requirement of God, that it was so small a matter as to render it marvellous that God should visit its violation with a penalty, we should remember that the smaller it was, the more readily ought obedience to have been rendered, and the greater the proof of a wrong disposition, when obedience was refused, even in a little thing.

2. The first wrong step is always marked by a peculiarity of evil which does not attach to any subsequent offence. Men are accustomed to palliate the first offence, because it is the first: a more accurate estimate would show that this habit of judging is thoroughly erroneous and fallacious. There is more to keep a man from committing a first offence, than there is to keep him from committing a second or any subsequent criminal act. The impression of the command is at least one degree deeper than it can possibly be after it has been trifled with. The first sin involves the taking up of a new position, and this is harder work than to maintain it. It is assuming a character of disobedience, and this requires more hardihood than to wear it when it has been once put on. It is breaking through consistency, which is a strong barrier so long as it is unbroken; but if once broken through, sin becomes easy. All these things call upon us, in fairness, to reverse our ordinary judgments on *first* offences; they suggest that these have an aggravation about them which belongs not to other sins; and we thus are the less surprised that God, whose every judgment is right, should have visited Saul's first offence with peculiar displeasure.

In the history thus reviewed there is a call for serious thought and prayerful enquiry on our own part. *Our own first sin,* absolutely considered, is a point beyond our recollection. The first sin which we ever committed, what was it? what was its form? when was it, and what was its date? It is in vain to ask, if we wait for a positive reply; and yet it is not in vain to give place to some solemn musings on the enquiry itself. There was a moment when our natural depravity first put itself forth into shape, so as to render us personally and actually guilty; and God recorded it in his book. Now if, neglecting the opportunity of a full and complete pardon provided for us through the atonement of the Son of God, we should, by reason of our own unbelief and folly, come into condemnation, *that sin* will be the first point in the divine judicial reckonings with us. The sentence of the judgment-seat of eternity will reach as far back as even to that. It is known to Omniscience; and in that dread day, when every secret will be discovered, it will be brought out to our view, and to our own melancholy recognition. Oh! fearful meeting between the unforgiven sinner and his first offence! Oh! who shall tell the anguish of that bitter recognition? Yet, on the other hand, if, through divine grace, we have heard and responded to the gracious message of reconciliation – if, pleading the interposition of Jesus, the Surety of the New Covenant, we have received pardon – then will our *first* sin define the extent to which that forgiveness has reached; it will be the point to which we refer when we seek in some adequate measure to form an experimental estimate of the riches of redeeming grace. And when, in heaven and throughout eternity, we sing the praises of the Lamb that was slain, our loudest notes will arise as we look back to this – the first offence which that blood washed away. Never let us forget that a time is coming when we shall meet – when we shall recognise, *our first sin,* our first wrong step. But how shall we meet it? pardoned or unforgiven? a witness against us for rejecting the Saviour, or a witness in favour of the exceeding great power of that blood which takes away all sin?

But there are sins which stand first in a relative sense, and these we can distinctly recollect. There was *that first departure,* Christian professor, after thou hadst taken upon thee solemn vows at the table of thy dying Lord. There was the first after thy renewed dedication to the Lord under circumstances peculiarly calculated to awaken holy love. There was the first after thou hadst come out of the furnace of affliction. There was the first after some most unexpected interposition of Divine Providence, which brought thee out of sorrow into comfort. These form grounds for humiliation – they cry aloud for self-abasement. As a means of producing contrition, and as affording motives for lying low in the dust of habitual repentance, the importance of frequently recalling them cannot be too highly estimated.

Yet others besides the professor have their first sins; and it would not be difficult for some to recall the first departure from the path of duty, after that serious illness which made them look eternity in the face; the first unlawful gratification after those solemn resolutions made in the moment of deep conviction; the first time they broke through the melting charge of their dying parent; the first time they ventured upon former worldliness after, to all appearance, they had determined to be the Lord's.

These first offences, to whatever class they belong, how should the remembrance of them fill us with gratitude at the divine forbearance. In the narrative of Saul we see God punishing the first offence. Nor is this the only instance in Scripture of the same kind. God did the same in Paradise, and He acted thus in accordance with every principle of justice. Why has He not done this with us? and where should we be now, if He had done so? "It is of the Lord's mercy that we are not consumed, and because his compassions fail not." May "the goodness of God lead us to repentance," and may that repentance show itself in holy caution. It is the *first offence* in any particular direction which Satan aims at inducing us to commit; that sin committed, the habit of doing right is broken through, and the next offence in the same direction will be easier. It is to this point that he addresses his most specious plea, "*Only this once.*" – "The first time, and it will be the last." But did it ever prove to be the last? All history says, No; and loud, among other evidence, is the testimony of the narrative of Saul.

Have we been brought into the right path, and tempted to forsake it, then be this our answer – "No! not even *the first* step will I venture again out of the path of duty. Why should I begin a course which I know to be wrong; of which I know not where it will end; and from which I may never be rescued?" Think of Saul's first wrong step, and pray, "Hold thou me up, and I shall be safe."

Chapter 5
Acting from Mere Impulse

"And the men of Israel were distressed that day: for Saul had adjured the people, saying, Cursed be the man that eateth any food until evening, that I may be avenged on mine enemies. So none of the people tasted any food ... And Jonathan told him, and said, I did but taste a little honey with the end of the rod that was in mine hand, and, lo, I must die. And Saul answered, God do so and more also: for thou shalt surely die, Jonathan." (*1 Samuel 14:24, 43, 44*)

TRUE religion has to do with much beyond the doctrines which a man holds; it demands that its professor should prove his sincerity by the life which he manifests, and the personal character which he bears. Hence we find that the first preachers of the gospel insisted quite as much upon the *conduct* which believers were to pursue as upon the *doctrines* which professors were to avow. Their view, as stated by the Apostle Paul, in writing to Titus, was this, "For the grace of God that bringeth salvation hath appeared to all men, teaching us that, denying ungodliness and worldly lusts, we should live soberly, righteously, and godly, in this present world; looking for that blessed hope, and the glorious appearing of the great God and our Saviour Jesus Christ; who gave himself for us, that he might redeem us from all iniquity, and purify unto himself a peculiar people, *zealous of good works.*" (*Titus 2:11-14*). We may conclude, therefore, that in the estimation of the primitive preachers of Christianity, the formal presentation of the doctrines of our holy religion, and the mere dwelling upon the historical facts associated with those doctrines, would not be "preaching the Gospel" in the fullest and most satisfactory sense of the term. And, further, that the habitual reference to points of conduct – holding up defects by way of caution, and describing what is excellent by way of example – is not only not inconsistent with gospel preaching, but that such a course ought always to constitute a main feature in the proclamation of divine truth. Now it is a fact worth noticing, that these first preachers, whom our Lord himself deputed to their work, while they dwelt largely upon matters of personal conduct, drew their illustrations, to a very considerable extent, from the Old Testament history. Its ancient narratives furnished instances for caution, and examples for imitation. *"All these things,"* said the Apostle Paul, after a very full reference to Old Testament facts, "happened unto them for ensamples: and they are written *for our admonition, upon whom the ends of the world are come."* (*1 Corinthians 10:11*). *They* held it, then, to be "preaching the Gospel" when they turned to the pages of this ancient volume, and dilated upon its histories; they evidently regarded the very reason of the preservation of these records to be, that they might be the means of conveying important instruction to the Church of God in later days. On this principle we may feel that when, in the ministrations of the sanctuary, the public expositors of God's truth are dwelling on the annals of the Old Testament – holding up, for the sake of admonition, the lives of men whose acts engaged the notice of generations long since passed away, or founding lessons of encouragement on the experience of others, whose names, ages ago, were like precious ointment, and which have lost none of their fragrance now – they are, nevertheless, in the scriptural sense of the term, "preaching the Gospel" – preaching it, as Paul did, as Peter did, in the days of their ministry, and as, doubtless, they would preach it still, if an earthly mission were again confided to them.

For the same reason, that the Gospel is concerned with the conduct and the life of individuals – that all its doctrines are designed to work in this direction, and to tell in this respect – it will be ours to feel that when, in our private studies of the holy Scriptures, we are occupied in the examination, for practical and experimental purposes, of any of these ancient biographies, we are carrying out the spirit of the Gospel, and using a most important means for producing a life and conversation worthy of a pure Christianity. The more deeply we are anxious to glorify our Divine Master, and with meekness and fear to maintain a holy life for His sake, the more valuable shall we deem any study which is calculated to throw light upon our personal duty, and the more willingly shall we commit ourselves to its pursuit.

In addressing ourselves, therefore, to that portion of Saul's history which succeeds his first wrong step, and which is recorded in *1 Samuel 14*, we have to propose the question, "What, in recording this passage, did the Holy Spirit mean that we should learn from it?" We shall not be long in perceiving that there is brought before us, chiefly, one more painful defect in Saul's general conduct, and that the consequences associated with that defect are very distinctly described: it is one, too, which is far from being uncommon, the results of which we are ourselves continually witnessing in a thousand varied forms. In codes of laws drawn up by man this defect is not indeed set down by name, and signalised as a sin, though humanity bleeds under its effects, but it is condemned, and justly so, by that "commandment" which is "exceeding broad." We refer to the habit of *inconsiderateness* – the habit of *acting from mere impulse,* of allowing merely momentary feeling to sway, without pausing to ask where the act which we perform, or the step on which we decide, will lead us, and how it will affect other persons besides ourselves. It is truly a melancholy instance which this chapter describes. It would appear that Jonathan and his armour-bearer had suddenly attacked one of the Philistine outposts – that God having interposed on their behalf, they succeeded in the skirmish – and dismay having taken hold of their adversaries, "the multitude melted away before them." Saul, seeing the advantage which had been gained, though without his intervention, assembled the people that they might pursue the Philistines; and, responding to his call, they came and "followed hard after them in the battle." But, not content with the simple course of action which was before him – that of following up an advantage for which he was indebted, under God, to the instrumentality of Jonathan, – he must needs commit an act of folly which is altogether unaccountable, except upon the principle that *self,* as a motive, is peculiarly blinding, and that a man who aims at self-glorification – at appearing *the important person* in an affair in which, really, he holds but a very secondary position, brings himself under an influence which will prevent or neutralise the power of other and wiser suggestions. So, having authority, Saul used it in putting forth a command that no one should taste any food until he had avenged himself of his enemies; nay, more, he invoked a curse upon the man who should transgress this most absurd and thoughtless decree, "Cursed be the man that eateth any food until evening." Accordingly, when, in their pursuit of the enemy, they met with food which would have invigorated them, wearied though they were with their exertions, they dared not taste it; and when, at length, having smitten the Philistines from Michmash to Aijalon, they became faint beyond endurance – they "flew upon the spoil, and took sheep, and oxen, and calves, and slew them on the ground: and" – what was strictly forbidden by the law – "the people did eat them with the blood," (*verse 32*). But this was not all: Jonathan was not there when his father uttered his most unwarrantable command, and therefore when, during the course of that fatiguing day, a supply of refreshment came most unexpectedly within his reach, he acted very differently from the rest of the people. "They came," says the narrative, "to a wood; and there was honey upon the ground. And when the people were come into the wood, behold, the honey dropped; but no man put his hand to his mouth: for the people feared the oath. But Jonathan heard not when his father charged the people with the oath: where-fore he put forth the end of the rod that was in his hand, and dipped it in an honeycomb, and put his hand to his mouth; and his eyes were enlightened." (*1 Samuel 14:25-27*). This circumstance of the honey being eaten by Jonathan, God employed as a means of exposing Saul's foolishness. The same evening, the priest was asking counsel of God as to the course which was to be pursued in refer-ence to the Philistines on the morrow, but no answer came. "Then," said the king, with that abrupt hastiness which had begun to mani-fest itself so painfully as a feature in his character, "then there must have been some sin committed; and though the offender were even Jonathan, my son, he shall surely die." Yes! and when the lot fell upon Jonathan, and the fact transpired that he, not knowing his father's decree, had tasted the honey, Saul still adhered to his sec-ond hasty determination, and he himself demanded the death of his own son, and would have insisted on the carrying out of his demand had not the people interposed, and rescued their favourite. True, indeed, were the words of Jonathan, "My father hath troubled

the land." (*14:29*). The interruption thus occasioned was most disappointing. The Philistines, who might have been destroyed, were
allowed to go to "their own place," to gather their forces for another
engagement, and the Israelites, displeased and vexed, returned to
their homes for a time. Such were the consequences of that one
thoughtless, reckless, rash sentence of Saul. To pronounce a curse at
all was presumptuous, where there was no direct command of God
to be infringed; and more, what personal pain it inflicted – what
actual disadvantages it involved – what further mischief it would
have done, if the matter had been left in the king of Israel's hand!
How different all would have been, if, instead of following the mere
impulse of an excited mind, he had thought for a moment, and,
when prompted to issue his decree, had paused to ask, How will
this affect my people? how will it operate in the end? But where, in
this imperfect world, can we turn our eyes without meeting scenes
and circumstances which cause us, involuntarily, to say within ourselves, "What a difference there would have been *here* if there had
been more of reflection and less of mere impulse." Nay, how many
passages in our own history, how many occurrences in our own life,
are most telling testimonies to ourselves of the evil of acting without staying to enquire into the bearing of what we do on our own
welfare, not to say on the feelings and comfort of others. Nothing
is more easy than to err through mere impulse; but in proportion
to the facility of doing wrong, in any one respect, is the duty of
being watchful and guarded on that very point. We may gather a
suggestion or two from this part of Saul's history, for our own caution and admonition.

1. Let us remember that this inconsiderateness, this acting from
mere impulse, is commonly the *result of an overweening regard to
self*. It was not Saul who commenced this engagement, but he could
not bear *not* to have the most prominent place in the affair, and he
must do something to make himself both seen and felt – he must
make his authority evident, though the result of his decree would
inevitably be the misery of his people all that day. His love for his
own dear self, and the manner in which all his thoughts centred
around that favourite object, are discernible in the very words of
the imprecation, "Cursed be the man that eateth any food until

evening, that *I* may be avenged on mine enemies." There were surely some higher, and more worthy and more forcible, motives for that day's work than just his own self-glorification – than the gratifying of his own wounded pride. If he had said, "That *my people* may be rid of their enemies; that the *kingdom of Israel* may be established; that *we* may be saved the inconveniences and the ruinousness of the perpetual incursions of these Philistines," – there would have been something honourable in the suggestion; but this "I – myself – I," how ill-timed it looks, how offensively it reads! To point out the evil is something towards ascertaining the remedy. Let us make the interests of others the object of our regard in all we undertake. Never let us think of ourselves without, at the same time, thinking of others too. Let us, as the apostle writes, "think of whatsoever things are lovely," (*Philippians 4:8*). The habit of attaching importance to others' convenience, to others' comforts, to others' feelings, will, under God, prove a great preservative against acting from mere impulse.

2. This habit, which we condemn, even though it may involve no serious consequences to others, is manifestly wrong, because it is decidedly *atheistic*. It affords no room for God; it makes no reference to Him. "In all thy ways acknowledge Him," is a command which needs no other basis than the simple fact that there is a God, and that we are His feeble and dependent creatures. When, on the spur of the moment, Nehemiah was asked by the monarch in whose presence he stood what he could do for him, though there did not appear any particular temptation to give a wrong answer, yet he did not venture to reply until he had prayed to the God of heaven. The enquiry came suddenly, but it was not answered without an application to the only source of wisdom for direction and guidance. But then Nehemiah was in the habit of associating God with everything, of putting Him in His proper place: Saul allowed Him perpetually to be out of sight. Hence the difference between the practice of the two men. The one acted deliberately, because he acted prayerfully; the other acted from impulse, because it was no part of his habit to recognise his dependence upon God.

3. Acting from impulse, while it often results in the infliction of mischief on others, is not less to be deprecated on account of the

injury which hasty and intemperate men occasion to themselves, and chiefly in this respect – the bitter and enduring bondage into which their thoughtlessness often brings them. The fact of having once committed themselves to a course, however erroneous, is often strangely used by men under Satan's power as a reason why they should continue in the same wrong path. The mental process involves three stages. There is the personal objection which every man feels to say that he has done wrong, though he may be quite conscious of the fact. Then there is the false notion of consistency, which men are often willing to maintain at any rate, as though *perseverance* in a questionable course *could neutralise its very questionableness* – as though the discredit of the action itself could be counterbalanced by the consistency with which it is carried out. And then there is, also, the continuance of the first impulse, which gives power to the other influences. Thus it comes to pass, that Satan holds a sway over the mind of the individual who makes his impulses his rule, in the same manner as he did over Saul, whom he would have induced, for a blind consistency's sake, even to have murdered his son; if, in the providence of God, a strong and determined hindrance had not been placed in his way, in the opposition of the people.

Think, then, before you act; *pray,* before you put your purpose into practice. Consider others as well as yourselves. Direct design to do wrong has slain its thousands; but the inconsiderateness of mere impulse has slain its tens of thousands. "None of us liveth to himself." Those rules for the family which, under God, better than any other would preserve its peace – those rules for the church which, more than anything besides, would maintain its union and its holiness – are these, "*Consider your ways,*" and "*Consider one another.*" Think of Jesus; think how He acted, how He reproved – "Ye know not what manner of spirit ye are of." Here, as everywhere, *prevention* is better than cure. Here, in truth, cure may often be entirely impossible. You may, indeed, repent of your want of thought – you may be forgiven, you may become altered in your habits, you may be more tender, more considerate, and more prayerful; but with all your prayers, and all your efforts, and all your tears, you may never be able to undo the mischief which one thoughtless act has done, nor heal the wounds which it has inflicted.

Beyond this special feature of instruction, the narrative allows us to draw some few general inferences as to the character of Saul's personal religion at this time.

1. It leads us to perceive how strangely partial his religion was in its operation. The faint and distressed state of the people led them, as soon as they had the opportunity, to "fly upon the spoil," and to eat the animals which they had slain "in their blood." This was against the ceremonial law which regulated matters of outward observance. And it being told Saul, he immediately took steps to prevent the continuance of this infringement of the ritual. So far, of course, he was right. But the eagerness with which he condemned the sin of the people in regard to a ceremonial omission – "Ye have transgressed," – contrasts strangely with the moral obtuseness which prevented him from seeing that his own folly had been the occasion of their sin. And we can hardly read his exhortation, "Sin not against the Lord in eating the blood," and find him a little afterwards actually determining to shed the blood of his own son, Jonathan, for not regarding an oath, of the existence of which he was perfectly ignorant, without coming to the conclusion that Saul's religion was not of a very deep character; that it was of that order which allows its professor to be vastly more affected by the neglect of something outward and formal than by the indulgence, within himself, of a wrong and impious state of mind. It puts us in mind of that most thorough manifestation of hypocrisy, of which the New Testament contains the record, when the accusers and betrayers of Jesus shrank back with sanctimonious step from the threshold of the judgment-hall, and would not set foot within it, "lest they should be defiled; but that they might eat the Passover." And yet, though their consciences would not allow them to do this, the very same consciences, when Pilate came out to them, and declared that Jesus was innocent, presented no obstacle to their murderous cry, "Crucify him – not this man, but Barabbas." It reminds us of that addition to the melancholy scene which occurred, when having, without compunction, passed by, and jeered, and wagged their heads at the sufferings of their victim, their scrupulosity was such, that they could not bear on their festival-sabbath that the body should remain on the cross; and they therefore besought Pilate that, the legs being broken, it should be taken away. Oh! strange admixture of

care for external proprieties with downright inward guilt; yet one which is full of instruction and admonition as to the dangers of that kind of religion which consists only in regard to forms and ceremonies. Nothing so blunts the moral sense, nothing so threateningly interferes with the right performance of the functions of conscience, as the idea that ceremonial acts, independently of holiness of heart, constitute real religion. And in these days of worldliness and formality, when every effort is being strained, by Popery avowed and Popery disguised, to insist on the value and meritoriousness, in the sight of God, of a rigid adherence to outward acts, we hold that it is our special duty to give serious attention to such cases as these to which reference has been made; calculated as they are to teach us that *high-toned morality declines just in proportion as mere ceremonial religion assumes the sway;* and that, if men really believe that the performance of certain outward acts and services is everything which is required of them, they will soon be ready to make light of gross violations of the law of Him who looketh not to the outward appearance, but trieth the hearts of His creatures.

2. Even in the discharge of proper religious duties, Saul was tardy and dilatory; and when, at last, he was found doing that which was right, he appeared to act, quite as much as when he did wrong, from mere impulse. On the occasion which suggests this remark we read, "And Saul built an altar unto the Lord;" and it is added, "The same was the first altar which he built unto the Lord." (*1 Samuel 14:35*). He had been king some time, he had received a great many mercies, had acquired honours, had gained victories, had known anxieties, but had also found relief and succour; but he *had never yet built an altar to the Lord,* as his own testimony on behalf of the God of Israel. And now that he did it, it appears probable that all at once and in a moment he conceived the idea of converting into an altar the great stone on which the animals used for food by the people had been slain. But that it should never have entered his mind to build an altar to God before, this was the point on which the Spirit of God directed that the sacred historian should pronounce emphatically. How keenly significant is that parenthetical sentence – "The same was the first altar which he built to the Lord!" It seems to say to us, God notices when you build the *first altar,* when you first set it

up, whether it be in the secret chamber or in the family. He knows the date of each secret religious transaction, keeps account when it was done, and how long an interval transpired before it was entered upon. The reflection may be very humiliating to many. It is a great mercy if, by God's grace, we have at length been persuaded to set up the altar *in our closet,* if we have begun to pray steadily and habitually; but does not our inmost heart still tell us, to our grief, that it might have been set up earlier? It was long, too long, before God looked and saw that it was there; but now we have it, let us guard it with a jealous eye. And it may have been long before we erected the *family* altar; many domestic blessings had been first received, but not acknowledged; many proofs of God's goodness afforded, but there had been no response; and we often think of the Divine patience in bearing with us during our neglect: but now we have it, let us keep it, let us dread nothing so much as that it should fall into decay. Let us not allow worldly engagements to interfere with private devotion, nor permit the presence of strangers, nor yet of unconverted friends, to cause an omission – *even for once* – of our domestic religion, of the exercises of family worship, lest *one* act of neglect should prove the precursor of the habit of indifference; and lest this, in its turn, should throw discredit on our profession, and plant our dying pillow with thorns. These thoughts lead us to a further notice of Saul's religion.

3. It was of a kind which allowed him to put God on one side, when he was too busy to attend to Him. This had been evident in the fact already adverted to; but another instance immediately follows. He was anxious to pursue the Philistines. "Let us go down," said he, "by night, and spoil them until the morning light, and let us not leave a man of them." The people assented; but a happier, holier suggestion was made by the priest – "Let us draw near hither unto God." But for this, the king would have gone, without any reference to God in the matter. He had, it is true, built an altar; but when he saw that the people had rested, and that there was a possibility of gaining a fresh advantage, he was for hurrying off, without the slightest thought of Divine guidance and counsel. There could not be a more affecting mark than this of his want of sincerity in religion. Real religion will ever put God *first* – *first,* as the Object whose glory is sought; and *first,* as the Being on whose aid we must, in the

spirit of humble dependence, rely. The multiplication of duties and engagements in this busy world may sometimes press heavily upon the religious professor; but at such seasons they really serve as tests of character. If he be truly what he professes to be, his sincerity will be seen in this, that he will not allow his busiest cares to interfere with fellowship with God – that everything will be made to give way to religion – and that religion will enter into every engagement; but if he be merely a professor, and nothing besides, you will discover his hollowness in this, that he will consent to religion when he has nothing else to do; but as sure as ever there comes some earthly advantage in the way, something particularly beneficial in his business pursuits, he will say, "Let me go – let me go!" and not stay for God's counsel and blessing.

4. With one more feature of Saul's religion we may close our study of the incidents of this chapter. It does not appear to have been characterised by the slightest self-suspicion, and there is consequently to be detected throughout, a singular want of humility. It never seems to have entered his thoughts that he could, by any possibility, have been in the wrong; but he was most ready to suppose that anyone else might be to blame. In the right direction of the lots as they were cast, it was the evident design of God to bring out to view the evil of Saul's inconsiderateness. He was the only culpable person, and God made that fact evident. Now, one would have thought that if anything could have brought him to a sense of his error, it would have been the discovery that his rash decree and oath had implicated his own son, Jonathan, in liability to suffering and death. But, no! he did not see it; he would not see it. Our indignation rises when we hear him say, "God do so and more also: for thou shalt surely die, Jonathan;" and we are ready to exclaim, "What! another oath? Has not one done mischief enough? cannot you see it? do you not feel it?" Nothing can exceed the hardening influence of that professed religion which leaves a man unsuspicious and ignorant of himself. History has told us, indeed, of fathers who have been constrained, in their judicial capacity, to pronounce sentence on their own children; but in such cases it has been done with a dignity which was impressive, and in a manner which showed that while the claims of law must be upheld, the feelings of the father were not lost in the act of the judge. But

here, Saul himself being the real transgressor, when he proceeded to pronounce sentence on Jonathan, there meets us a manifestation of conduct so cold, so coarse, that we turn away in disgust, or stay to give our hearts the relief of joining in the indignant cry which dared the inhuman parent to carry out his purpose, "Shall Jonathan die? God forbid: as the Lord liveth, there shall not one hair of his head fall to the ground; for he hath wrought with God this day." What are we when left to ourselves? How blind to ourselves – how mischievous to others! What warnings we can neglect – what just cause for humiliation we can evade!

Be it ours, then, by means of a diligent and prayerful study of the Scriptures, to aim at the detection of those features of character which are hateful to God, and which must be avoided, if we would so walk as to please Him. Let us feel, too, the rich satisfaction of being able to turn from aspects of character which are distressing, to the life of One in whose example we shall find the actual opposites of them all, and in whose death, as a proof of love to us, we shall discover the strongest motive to manifest, in our own conduct, what we admire in Him. Well will it be, if the very necessity of turning away in pain from man, brings with it the desire and delight of "looking to Jesus." And, once more, let the "first altar" which Saul set up prove a source of instruction to ourselves. Many who read these pages may not have their "first altar" to set up – that was done long ago; but it may be, that if the question were asked, "*Where is that altar now?*" some could only give a reply which it would be as painful to receive as it would be humiliating to utter. Time was, when, regularly as the morning dawned, and punctually as the sun went down, that altar was frequented, but this is the case no longer. The signs of domestic religion, of the uniting and sanctifying acts of family devotion would now be looked for in vain, and with their disappearance have failed other evidences of personal religion. Ah! with what reason God can complain of – with what justice, too, could He visit for – these things! And visit He will, except there be repentance and reform. Does conscience never hear the whispers of a future judgment, which will call you to account? if not of some nearer judgment which will prove that the way to lose comfort, peace, and honour, is to lose God's blessing, and that the way to lose God's blessing is to neglect God's altar. Be wise in time. Set up afresh that altar which now lies in ruins; go, kneel beside it – bedew it with your tears, and then let the evening of the day which will thus prove the season of personal repentance witness your household assembled, at your invitation, as in days of old. You need not explain; your act will be significant enough: they will feel, they will understand; and God will understand and approve it too.

There may be other readers, of whom it could not be said that they have ever built even their "first altar" to the Lord. They are strangers to real devotion. They may sometimes bend the knee, and repeat the language of supplication which they do not feel, but they have no stated habit of prayer, of personal communion with God. How long shall this neglect continue? Is not the same God who noticed Saul's delay now recording yours? And will there not be a heavier condemnation in your case than in his? Many a circumstance, to which Saul was a stranger, might act within your bosoms as an incentive to habits of prayer – the knowledge of the great High Priest, of His alone-sufficient sacrifice, of His gracious promises, of His assured advocacy. The failure to set up the altar of private devotion implies that these motives are treated as nullities; but can this be safely done? If thus disregarded, will they not turn to the condemnation of those who have not set up their "first altar?"

There is a class of individuals, however, who could tell of the altar they have set up for themselves, but who could give no satisfactory reply, if the enquiry proceeded a single point beyond themselves. Their families never have an opportunity of surrounding that altar – the first act of household religion has yet to be performed. Heads of families, yourselves the recipients of a thousand mercies, who have lived years together in outward comfort and in social respectability, if conscience testifies to this failure, hasten, in divine strength, to act on the determination that there shall no longer be wanting this hallowed recognition of God in your homes. Especially, let this most striking record of Saul's "first altar" serve as a touching appeal to those who have just entered upon houses of their own. Husbands – wives – experiencing at this very hour how much of earth's purest joys God has connected with the relation in which you stand to each other – would you preserve that joy, would you have it increase and abound? – you are going the wrong way if you have not set up "the first altar" to God in your houses. Oh! keep Him not waiting for this mark of reverence, this proof of felt dependence. Begin on principle, and not from impulse. Begin from a loving view of God, mingled with humility and contrition; and be assured that, as God is true, blessings will await you, rich and effectual blessings, in fulfilment of His gracious promise, "Blessed is every one that feareth the Lord; that walketh in His ways. For thou shalt eat the labour of thine hands: happy shalt thou be, and it shall be well with thee ... Behold, that thus shall the man be blessed that feareth the Lord." (*Psalm 128:1, 2, 4*).

Chapter 6

"What meaneth then this bleating of the sheep in mine ears?"

"And Samuel came to Saul: and Saul said unto him, Blessed be thou of the Lord: I have performed the commandment of the Lord. And Samuel said, What meaneth then this bleating of the sheep in mine ears, and the lowing of the oxen which I hear?" (*1 Samuel 15:13, 14*)

MEN sometimes speak of God as though He were harsh and unrelenting. They invest Him – and if ever men do Satan's work, it is when this is their employment – they invest Him with those attributes of character which belong to a person in a state of excitement or of irritation; and they are ready to ascribe the destruction which is the portion of the sinner, rather to some defect in the Being who inflicts the penalty, than to any guilt which attaches to the rebel on whom the sentence falls. They represent God as being less merciful than man; the Creator as being less indulgent, less forbearing, than the creature. But is it so? There is one order of dispensation which contradicts such a view, and with a most decided emphasis; and it is this course of dealing on the part of God to which we are conducted by that portion of the narrative of Saul which comes next in order before us. Do harshness and relentlessness show themselves in granting space for repentance where offence has been committed – where it has been repeated – where it has evidently passed into

the habit of wrong-doing –in giving a further opportunity for obedience – *one trial more* – which, thankfully embraced and humbly
employed, might issue in proof being furnished of true repentance,
and so might afford ground for the reversal of the sentence which had
already been announced and fully deserved? Yet such is the course of
Divine Providence which the incidents now before us indicate. Time
had passed on since Saul's first public offence had brought upon him
the displeasure of God. But he still held the kingdom; it had not been
visibly rent from him. And now it was to be seen what effect had been
produced upon his mind by the messages which God had sent, the
threatenings which He had uttered, and the forbearance which He
had shown. God would put him once more to the test, would require
of him one more simple act of obedience, and at the same time would
afford him every opportunity of manifesting it.

He therefore sent the prophet with this command, "Thus saith the
Lord of hosts, I remember that which Amalek did to Israel, how he
laid wait for him in the way, when he came up from Egypt. Now go
and smite Amalek, and utterly destroy all that they have, and spare
them not; but slay both man and woman, infant and suckling, ox and
sheep, camel and ass." (*15:2, 3*). How fully Samuel appreciated the
mercy implied in this trial of obedience, how deeply anxious he was
that Saul should obey, how earnest that he should not throw away this
opportunity of pleasing God, and of manifesting repentance for past
folly, is testified by the imploring manner with which he delivered his
message, the fervent preface with which he opened it – "Samuel also
said unto Saul, The Lord sent me to anoint thee to be king over his
people, over Israel: now therefore hearken thou unto the voice of the
words of the Lord." (*15:1*). It was like saying, Do be obedient *this time,*
do not throw away *this* opportunity, do not trifle with *this* command.

And what did Saul? The tenor of the narrative inevitably excites a
renewal of those feelings of disappointment which have so frequently
been called up by the study of this history, for it brings before us
another instance of the most strange and wilful disobedience.
Nothing could be more clear than the definition of the duty, nothing more decisively marked out than the thing which God required
Saul to do. But a course of action more certainly calculated to insult
the majesty of Heaven cannot be conceived than that which Saul
adopted. It is true the command was partially obeyed, but the only

case in which obedience was rendered was that in which there was no temptation to gratify selfish feeling. Where, however, anything could be turned to his own personal advantage, there the command of God was recklessly trifled with.

There are mysteries in grace; but most assuredly there are mysteries in sin, too, which only the Bible enables us to clear up; strange contradictions in the courses of wicked men; passages which would be perfectly puzzling, if it were not for the light thrown on them by God's Word. Look attentively at Saul in this matter. When Jonathan had done nothing to deserve death, when to have visited him with this penalty would have been a direct infringement of God's command, "Thou shalt not kill," there was no mercy for him – as we saw in the preceding chapter – no mercy for him in his father's heart; and it required the downright and peremptory prohibition of all Saul's army to save the innocent son alive. But when a duty was rendered imperative by that God who is not bound to give, in any case, his reasons for action – who does afford them in some instances, but who always has them, and of the best and most sufficient order – when, by God himself, Saul was deputed to put Agag to death, when to have done this would have been but an act of simple obedience, he ventured to disobey, and spared the man whom God had marked for destruction. We are staggered by this, except as we listen to the voice of Scripture, which declares the enmity of the carnal heart against God. That inspired affirmation is but another form of telling us that man likes his own way best; that, if there be more to gratify self in the course which God has forbidden than in that which He has prescribed, man has a heart which will nullify the precept and dare to break through the prohibition. It was, in Saul's view, a matter of pride to have his triumph graced by the presence of a conquered king, to make Agag feel that he owed his life to his own clemency, and that he held its prolongation on the tenure of his conqueror's will. He found a greater gratification in all this than in simple obedience to God. But in connection with this act, we find recorded a circumstance which stamps his character yet more deeply with unworthiness, with a mean selfishness which makes us recoil as we trace its forbidding development. It is added, that he also spared "the best of the sheep, and of the oxen, and of the fatlings, and the lambs, and all that was good, and would not utterly destroy them: but everything that was vile and refuse, that they destroyed utterly." (*15:9*). The time was at length come when God – who had forborne so long, who had waited so patiently, who had given another opportunity of obedience, only, indeed, to be trifled with and lost – the time had come when He would mark His sense of the rebellion and ingratitude with which His mercy had been followed. "It repenteth me," said He, "that I have made Saul to be king," (*15:11*); an utterance which must not be taken in any sense at variance with the Divine immutability and foreknowledge, but simply as a condescending adoption of an expression which men employ when they are about to change their course of action – and intended to prepare the prophet's mind for announcing to Saul the intelligence of his altered position. Samuel goes, after a night spent in grief and in prayer, to be the bearer of the tidings of God's displeasure. But what strange scene is this which breaks upon us as the messenger of the Lord reaches Gilgal? Much as we know of Saul, and accustomed as we have become to the proofs of his moral obtuseness, we are hardly prepared for the downright self-complacency, for the cool effrontery of the words which he addressed to Samuel, "Blessed be thou of the Lord: I have performed the commandment of the Lord," (*15:13*); and we feel the justice of the grave and searching enquiry, "What meaneth then this bleating of the sheep in mine ears, and the lowing of the oxen which I hear?" (*15:14*). The interview so vividly sketched invites us to pause, and take advantage of some of its obvious suggestions.

I. We are reminded that a great amount of direct sin may be committed, and nevertheless disguised, under a loud profession of obedience to God. There is, in some individuals, a forwardness in certain forms of duty which cost no self-denial at all; a forwardness, also, in the announcement of what has been done which is, in itself, to practised eyes a ground for suspicion that all is not right behind the scenes. The very fervour of that greeting, addressed to the man whose duty it was to be faithful, suggested that there was something wrong beneath it. You see, at once, that it was intended either to blind or to disarm the prophet. And as a piece of policy, it is eminently worthy of observation. We sometimes notice individuals overdoing the thing that is courteous and polite – "glaringly civil" – towards those who come on the errand of Christian fidelity, and whose business is with souls in prospect of the great account. There is so much joy expressed at seeing them, there is so much interest taken in their presence, there is such a sudden burst of cordiality, as that upon the very amazement excited there follows the suspicion that something is going on which there is an effort to conceal. Or if, as in Samuel's case, that something wrong is already known, this superabundant courtesy will ever produce a holy indignation at the attempt to tamper with personal and official fidelity, and will ever lead sincere servants of God to think only of Him whose they are and whom they serve, and to ask, as Samuel did, "What meaneth then this bleating of the sheep in mine ears?" Do we plead for consistency in a religious profession, we cannot more fully express and describe the kind of religion which alone will be pleasing to God, and with nothing short of which the Church or its ministers should be satisfied, than by calling attention to Saul's conduct in this matter, and by warning against anything which would be like "the bleating of the sheep" in contrast with the profession of Saul's entire obedience, or with the warmth of his greeting when he met the prophet, conscious as he was of his short-coming. Let us aim after such a walk and conversation as that we can be natural in our demeanour, and not artificial and forced; such a life as will bear inspection behind the scenes, and as will not compel those who watch for souls to ask, as they look around, *what meaneth this or that?* what meaneth this unholy gratification? what meaneth this unsubdued temper? what meaneth this unlovely spirit? what meaneth this worldly conformity? and while asking the question to feel the sad truth of the matter to be, that the thing which calls forth the question is in our case, as it was in Saul's, only so much spared of that which God has commanded us to subdue and destroy, so much permitted to live which God had required us to conquer and to slay.

II. But mark the answer of Saul; let those mark it, especially, who are young, and who are exposed, because they are young, to peculiar temptations by which men who do Satan's work strive to lead away unwary souls; let them mark it, because it teaches them that the men who, to gratify their own purposes, will lead them wrong and countenance them in evil-doing, will be the very first to expose them when they want to excuse themselves. "And Saul said, '*They,*'" – not *I* – "*they* have brought them from the Amalekites: for *the people* spared the best of the sheep and of the oxen, to sacrifice unto the Lord thy God; and the rest we have utterly destroyed." (*15:15*). Ah! study well that sentence, "they" *did it.* Would that its impressiveness might be felt by the thousands who are too ready to be led by the advice, by the example, of those who ought to have but one rule for their own conduct and for their influence over others too, and that rule *God's Word – God's will.* Alas! that in this wicked world there should be those who have a direct influence in making you sin, and in rendering its commission easy for you. There are those whose worldly, whose pecuniary interests lie in the existence and perpetuation of wicked courses. There are some who will lead you into evil for the sake of getting countenance to themselves in their own want of religion. There are others who would like to overthrow religion altogether, and whose delight would be to diminish the number of Christ's disciples in a district or locality, and they aim at bringing about this result by enticing the young from the ways of holiness, by offering them the opportunity – accompanied by the promise of concealment – of gratifying unholy desires and worldly feelings. But are these your real friends? How often, on the contrary, have melancholy instances proved that these tempters are the first to expose their victims, the very first to throw the entire blame off themselves and upon those whom they have led astray. How many have had to mourn at last, when they have found their advisers converted into their accusers, when they have seen their companions in guilt stand as the witnesses for their condemnation. No! they are not your friends, but rather your worst enemies, who tempt – who facilitate – who stand by, and let you sin. "My son, if sinners entice thee, consent thou not." (*Proverbs 1:10*).

III. There are some other points to be observed – other erroneous principles in this answer of Saul.

1. He evidently implied that a *formal* act of obedience might be taken as a set-off against an act of direct disobedience. He pleaded that these sheep, these oxen, had been spared that they might be sacrificed unto the Lord. He admitted that the command had not been fulfilled literally, but that this omission was with a view of doing what must be acceptable to God; and that the splendid sacrifices which he and the people were about to offer would be quite an equivalent for the defect of his literal disobedience, if indeed they did not go much

further than to compensate for that defect. He implied that, putting one thing over against the other, God would be satisfied in the long run. As though an end, good in itself, could ever justify unhallowed means for securing it; as though anything could ever warrant a direct contravention of God's positive command; as though an act of an outward kind, however proper in its own form, could please God when it was attended by and associated with a state of mind which was in undoubted opposition to his express direction. We do not, of course, believe – who would? who could? – that Saul told the whole truth, and nothing but the truth, when he assigned this reason for sparing the spoil of the Amalekites. If he intended to offer sacrifice at all, it was upon the principle of compromise and composition. He would have given God a part of the spoil, that he might have kept a much larger portion for himself. He would have offered a fraction, that the extensive remainder might not have rendered his conscience uneasy. For men will do this; and it is strange to see how, when conscience has been tampered with, though it be not quite asleep, a very fragment given to God of their possessions, by whatever means obtained, will leave men satisfied to withhold from Him all the rest.

The prophet took Saul upon his own showing, and his answer was on this wise: "Admitting that it is as you say, that in sparing this spoil your object was to sacrifice unto the Lord, yet has the Lord as great delight in burnt-offerings and sacrifices, as in obeying the voice of the Lord? Behold, to obey is better than sacrifice, and to hearken than the fat of rams." In those sacrifices which you offer to God no equivalent is found for the want of obedience. If outward service, indeed, were valuable for its own sake – if it were, in every respect, of the same value as the obedience of the heart and the dedication of its powers and dispositions to the carrying out of God's will – *then* indeed, and *only then,* could the lack of the one be made up by the presentation of the other – then only could the offering of outward service make compensation for the want of a right state of mind. But the prophet argues that it is not so. Obedience, as a principle, has a value far above sacrifice, as an action; *it is "better than sacrifice"* – better, as the principle must be superior to the form in which it is embodied – better, as the affection which sends a gift is more valuable than the gift itself. How, then, with justice, can the one be substituted for the other? How, then, can God accept the inferior as a compromise for the absence of that which in every sense is *better,* and which alone gives any worthiness to the inferior and external? "Hath the Lord as great delight in burnt-offerings and sacrifices, as in obeying the voice of the *Lord?*"

The offering and the sacrifice have a value as embodiments of the principle of obedience and love – *then only* are they acceptable; but as substitutes for principle they have no acceptableness in the estimation of Him, who is at once the Searcher of hearts and the great Proprietor of all; and who – when the attempt is made to put Him off, so to speak, with the inferior for the superior, with the external for the spiritual, with the form for the reality – can utter with indignant tones His own mind and His own principles of action thus: "I will not reprove thee for thy sacrifices or thy burnt-offerings to have been continually before me." It is not for these I blame thee, but for thy resting satisfied with these; and for expecting that I should rest satisfied in the absence of a right and grateful spirit, as originating them and represented by them. These sacrifices, for their own sake, I do not want. "I will take no bullock out of thy house, nor he-goats out of thy folds. For every beast of the forest is mine, and the cattle upon a thousand hills. I know all the fowls of the mountains: and the wild beasts of the field are mine. If I were hungry, I would not tell thee; for the world is mine, and the fulness thereof. Will I eat the flesh of bulls, or drink the blood of goats? Offer unto the Lord thanksgiving." Let there be beneath all this exterior the spirit of gratitude showing itself in obedience and love, "and pay thy vows," fulfil thy holy pledges and solemn acts of personal, spiritual consecration "unto the Most High." (*Psalm 50:9-14*). And where is the thoughtful reader of this narrative who will not admit that these lessons on the distinction between *the form* and *the reality* of religion are as necessary in the present day as they were in the age of Samuel and Saul?

2. Another error in Saul's answer to which Samuel addressed himself was this, that, *admitting he was in fault, there was no great harm in his sin after all.* The king of Israel did not, indeed, use these words, but doubtless the prophet gathered that this was his real sentiment, as well from the manner in which he spoke, as from the tenor of what he said; for the narrative presents him as going on to combat exactly this view, that if the thing which he had done were wrong

– it was but a trifling act, and need not be so severely noticed. He declares that a sin which, to the eye of man, may not seem to have about itself any particular or special enormity, may be, in the sight of God, just as bad, just as abhorred as any one of those sins which not only God's Word denounces, but against which public opinion would rise for the purpose of condemning them: "For rebellion is as the sin of witchcraft, and stubbornness is as iniquity and idolatry." Here we see a class of sins mentioned whose heinousness was undoubted. *Witchcraft* God had forbidden to be tolerated on any account. *Iniquity* is here undoubtedly put for flagrant violation of God's law; such, for instance, as the idolatry mentioned immediately after. The probability is that the king of Israel plumed and prided himself upon his public acts in reference to these very points; that having found it convenient, for the maintenance of his official position, to preserve an outward regard to religion, he had set himself against the worship of idols; and that, being afraid of some unwelcome consequences to himself from the arts of witchcraft, he had put away out of the land those who professed to have familiar spirits; and that, having acquired some reputation to himself from these acts, he had laid the flattering unction to his soul of being the firm opponent of witchcraft and idolatry. And now, how keen the rebuke – You have acted as though you thought witchcraft was a great crime, and so it is; but then rebellion such as that which you have manifested is as bad. Witchcraft is displeasing to God, and implies the putting of something else in the place which belongs to Him; it is the appeal to another power in a province in which He has sole jurisdiction: and your rebellion, what has that been but putting God out of His proper place of authority, and consulting your own will and your own inclination instead of listening to His voice. You have acted as though you thought that idolatry was a fearful offence, an awful manifestation of iniquity against God, and so it is; but then stubbornness like that which you have displayed is just as evil, for it is a refusal on your part to bow down to the only proper object of supreme regard; it is making self your god, and saying to the Most High, "Depart from me; I desire not the knowledge of thy ways." (*Job 21:14*). Outwardly, the things look differently; but really, and as far as principle is concerned, they are identical. Thou, therefore, that teachest another, thou shalt not consult wizards, because it is an insult to the God of Israel, the only proper guide of His people – dost thou insult Him, too, by asking counsel of thine own weak and foolish heart? Thou that sayest, Thou shalt not worship idols; thou shalt worship the Lord thy God, and Him only shalt thou serve – dost thou, by thine obstinacy and stubbornness, deny the claims of God, and make an idol of thine own self?

We shall not in vain have studied this passage in Saul's history, if there be secured in our hearts a place for this lesson – *that the actual amount of our guilt must not be adjusted by the external form of the transgression in which it issues – by its classification according to outward appearance.* Saul congratulated himself on being thought far superior to the consulter of those who had familiar spirits, and would have been shocked at the idea of being regarded as an idolater; but God thought him just as bad as though he were the one or the other, for in fact he was both in the spiritual classification of Him in whose sight "all things are naked and open." It is well for us to recollect, that in spirit we may be bearing the very same kind of guilt before the eye of Omniscience, which we are condemning in the declared conduct of others. It is well to recollect, that in the view of God we may be just outraging the very same principle, the infringement of which by others we are visiting with our severest censure – to recollect that, as God reads, we may be standing side by side with the criminals whose judges we vainly fancy ourselves to be. Ask not, then, simply of your outward life, but enquire of your inward principles; ask not what estimate man forms of you, but what position God's classification, according to real character, assigns to you. Ask not, simply, Am I free from this sin, or that, as man reads me? but, Am I free from it, as God surveys me? For, as this passage tells us, that there were more ways than one of being guilty of the sins of witchcraft and idolatry, so it is equally true of other sins – whether of impurity, or dishonesty, or Sabbath-breaking, or any violation of divine law – there are more ways than one of committing each of them, and there may be the guilt of either of them incurred, though man may never observe or find it out. "Thou that preachest a man should not steal," dost thou steal? though under another form. "Thou that sayest a man should not commit adultery," art thou guilty of any kind of impurity in heart? "Thou that makest thy boast of the law, through breaking the law," in any form, "dishonourest thou God?" "Therefore thou art inexcusable, O man, whosoever thou art, that judgest; for wherein thou judgest another, thou condemnest thyself: for thou that judgest doest the same things. But we are sure that the judgment of God is according to truth against those which commit such things. And thinkest thou this, O man, that judgest those which do such things, and doest the same, that thou shalt escape the judgment of God?" (*Romans 2:1-3*).

It forms a special ground for caution, in regard to the point on which we have been insisting, that we discover that it received a further but a singular illustration in the history of Saul. Did his spirit rise up against being thought as bad in his rebellion as if he had patronised witchcraft and sought those who had familiar spirits? Did the prophet's word seem bold when he classified him, according to principle, with those from whom he professed to stand aloof? He lived to give, in his own person, the painful but the clearest evidence of the identity, as far as concerns a common origin and principle of action, which may exist between two very different crimes; for under the influence of the very class of feelings, which led him at one time to his own indulged course of sin, he at length proceeded to the actual commission of that crime which he publicly and officially condemned in others. He who had professedly recoiled from witchcraft, went himself to consult a witch. The same disposition which evidenced itself in those acts of rebellion which he committed all the while that he was crying down witchcraft, induced him to do the thing which he publicly censured when the temptation pressed, and when it answered his purpose to do it. Let this circumstance speak trumpet-tongued, and let it say, You may live to do yourself the very thing you condemn in another; there may be lurking in your heart the principle which will lead to the very same form of sin which at present you stoutly condemn. In a word, let us bear in mind that the security against our being guilty of any particular form of transgression is not that we condemn it, but that we have the evil principle within us, which excites to its commission, subdued and removed by divine grace. The only security against *any* sin is the implantation of that holiness which teaches us to hate *all* evil.

We have spoken of the present classification of transgressions by God as a Spirit; let us remember that a day is coming which will be distinguished by an outward and visible classification, in which He will be the immediate Agent; and this will be a final and an irrevocable act. In that great day where shall we stand? By that decisive act, what position will be assigned us? All then will turn on principle, and not on outward form – on what *God has seen,* not on what *man has thought.* Then there will be but two classes – the one defined by the principle of supreme love to God through Jesus Christ, of love so supreme that for His sake, and for the sake of that dear Son whom He sent into the world, it would give up *all* that was displeasing to Him, and rather than grieve Him would cut off the right hand, or pluck out the right eye, if these proved the occasions of offence; the other class constituted of those who, though under varied forms, some more public and some more private, yet lived to give the painful proof that the love of God was not the ruling principle of their life. The mingling together of individuals then, no longer according to their outward character, but according to their inward and spiritual life – in what strange allocations and associations will it issue! How many, who prided themselves on the outward decorousness of their walk, will be amazed to find that, because there was as little *real* religion in their formality as in the manifest irreligion of others, the two must stand side by side! How many then, like Saul, will learn the lesson, though with grievous variations, which the prophet's language of rebuke conveyed! How many will be overwhelmed to see that the angry thoughts, the feelings of animosity, which they indulged, but which they never acted out because they feared consequences, are yet reckoned as specific deeds; and that they stand along with those who have put forth their evil dispositions in palpable forms! How many will be amazed to find that the covetousness, which induced them to pursue the world, and to make it their idol, issues in their being ranked with those who made a graven image, and bowed down to it, and said, "Deliver us, for thou art our God!" May our hearts be quickened by these reflections, and the springs of our actions be renewed and purified. May our obedience be more willing, more principled. Feeling our own weakness, and impressed with God's omniscience, let this be our prayer, Create in me a clean heart, O God! renew a right spirit in me. "Behold, thou desirest truth in the inner parts: and in the hidden part thou shalt make me to know wisdom."

Chapter 7

National Sins and National Punishments

"Thus saith the Lord of hosts, I remember that which Amalek did to Israel, how he laid wait for him in the way, when he came up from Egypt. Now go and smite Amalek, and utterly destroy all that they have." (*1 Samuel 15:2, 3*)

THIS command addressed to Saul has claims on our attention for important reasons, beyond those which have already been suggested in the preceding pages. It there came before us as a solemn call from God for the performance of an act of unqualified obedience. We saw divine forbearance giving an offender one trial more, one opportunity more, of manifesting a right state of mind. But the opportunity was thrown away, the trial only served to indicate the still hardened and rebellious spirit of Saul; and deaf to the expostulations of Samuel, and blind to his own best interests, he displayed a mournful consistency with those his former sinful habits which had already brought on him the merited displeasure of the Most High.

But apart from the consideration of that act which God required, viewed as a test of Saul's state of mind, the manner in which the expedition against the Amalekites is announced, and the reasons assigned for its being proposed, conspire to throw around the mission itself a deep interest, constraining us to study the matter, and promising to repay our investigation. We turn, then, for a moment, from Saul to the case of those against whom he was sent. "Thus saith the Lord of hosts, I remember that which Amalek did to Israel, how he laid wait for him in the way, when he came up from Egypt." Then God does remember sin. He not only notices it, but remembers it. A lengthened period had transpired since the Amalekites had thus manifested their sympathy with the enemies of Israel, by throwing hindrances in the way of God's chosen people as they came out of Egypt to Canaan. And, to all appearance, their sin might have been regarded as consigned to oblivion. But God had declared that it should not be forgotten. There was something not only so cruel in the attack upon the Hebrew tribes, when they had scarcely recovered from the toils and perils immediately associated with their escape from the land of bondage, but so daring in the effort to crush those for whom God had so signally interposed, that the Most High felt the affront to be deep, the insult to be monstrous; and while He interfered to protect His people, He proceeded, in a most impressive form, to mark His sense of this national crime – "And the Lord said unto Moses, Write this for a memorial in a book, and rehearse it in the ears of Joshua: for I will utterly put out the remembrance of Amalek from under heaven." (*Exodus 17:14*). And once more we find the solemn charge given to Israel, proving how God regarded the attack of this nation upon His own people as a crime of high degree against Himself – "Remember what Amalek did unto thee by the way, when ye were come forth out of Egypt; how he met thee by the way, and smote the hindmost of thee, even all that were feeble behind thee, when thou wast faint and weary; and he feared not God. Therefore it shall be, when the Lord thy God hath given thee rest from all thine enemies round about, in the land which the Lord thy God giveth thee for an inheritance to possess it, that thou shalt blot out the remembrance of Amalek from under heaven; thou shalt not forget it." (*Deuteronomy 25:17-19*). Yet it looked as though this had not operated as a motive during the days of the Judges. No special notice is taken of the sin which had defied the God of heaven – the daring act by which one nation bared its arm, and raised its hand to encounter that God who had just taught another, and a powerful nation too, that "none ever hardened himself against God, and prospered." The discomfiture which the Amalekites had received at the time of their actual assaults in the wilderness had ceased to be impressive; and if the tidings had ever reached them that wrath was reserved for them in the future by Him whose rod they had once felt, the last whispers of that prediction had either died away, or lingered only as a tradition which they could afford, in their fancied security, to laugh at. And now, upon the oblivion of four centuries, there broke the awful tones of Almighty Justice: "I remember that which Amalek did." From that Infinite Mind there had been no obliteration of the crime; clear as on the day on which it had been committed, that sin stood out to view. "*I remember.*" Divine forbearance with generation after generation had been long, but upon them that forbearance had been lost, and it is evident they had not profited by it. They still remained the foes of Israel; their conduct as a nation was marked by excessive cruelty; and it was a horrible notoriety which their king had obtained for the multitudes of mothers whom, in his blood-thirstiness, his sword had rendered childless.

In the determination on the part of God now to punish, the utterance of which was prefaced by those emphatic words, "I remember," we are distinctly taught the lesson that the conduct of nations is a point to which the eye of God is directed, and that it is the matter for which His just penalty will be reserved. Whole nations come within the compass of His gaze, and within the reach of His rod. By the *individuals* composing a community, and whose personal welfare or woe is necessarily identified with the condition of the community, there is a great danger that national sin should be regarded rather as an abstraction than as a reality, rather as *an ideal* than a substantial criminality. But it is not thus that God, in the incident before us, deals with it. He affixes it, as a substantive charge, upon the community. And He who did thus with the daring impiety of Amalek, who marked it and recorded it, has ever done the same with the sins of other nations; and as, one after another, their greatness has tottered and fallen, the sun of their prosperity declining and setting behind the clouds of desolation and destruction – amidst the solitude which has reigned in their ruined cities and the lull of the tempest which has swept over their sites – there has, ever and anon, been heard, by the thoughtful traveller and the attentive reader of the past and the present, the still, small voice from the unseen world which has explained it all – "I remember that which they did." We have a rule here to which we find no exception. But nowhere does this rule meet with so fearful an exemplification as in the case of that very people whose guardian God showed Himself to be in this act of visiting Amalek's transgression

– that very Israel on whose behalf He was now standing up to repel insult and to avenge injury. Selected as the object of special divine favour – brought by His own sovereign act into a peculiarly close relationship to Himself – gifted with the opportunity of proving what national religion might be, and what national blessings would follow in the train of such a manifested religion – when these favours were slighted, these opportunities thrown away, this very people became, in the hands of a just and jealous God, a warning that it is dangerous for nations to provoke divine displeasure. "*I remember*" – read it in those seventy years' exile from the land which had been given for an inheritance – that long and dreary period, during which Zion's history was thus announced in plaintive tones by the prophet, "How doth the city sit solitary, that was full of people! how is she become as a widow! she that was great among the nations, and princess among the provinces: how is she become tributary!" (*Lamentations 1:1*). "Her gates are sunk into the ground; He hath destroyed and broken her bars: her king and her princes are among the Gentiles: the law is no more; her prophets also find no vision from the Lord." (*Lamentations 2:9*). "*I remember*" – read it in those tremendous forms in which God visited that "swearing" on account of which "the land mourned," that "oppression" on account of which prophets lifted up their voice, that "uncleanness" which God's message reproved, that "Sabbath-breaking," that "drunkenness," over which the "ministers of the Lord" wept "between the porch and the altar." "*I remember*" – read it in its reiterated and doubly-telling tones in that second destruction which succeeded a second opportunity given to the Hebrew people of a sound national repentance and reformation – that second opportunity which was lost when formalism was substituted for spiritual religion; when beneath outwardly decent appearance, corruption reigned uncontrolled, and the "whited sepulchre full of dead men's bones" became but too true an emblem of the actual condition of the religious guides of the people; and when all sin, all unbelief, all ingratitude, all cruelty, were concentrated in that one act at which the very rocks quaked, that one unparalleled act of atrocity from which the sun withdrew his light – the rejection of the Son of God, the putting to death of the Lord of Life and Glory. Hark to the words of mingled compassion and judgment which fall from His lips as He stands over against the city and weeps, "O Jerusalem, Jerusalem, thou that killest the prophets, and stonest them which are sent unto thee, how often would I have gathered thy children together, even as a hen gathereth her chickens under her wings, and ye would not! Behold your house is left unto you desolate." (*Matthew 23:37, 38*). Yes, and in that desolation, as it still remains – in those still mourning ways of Zion, and in those "tribes of the weary foot and trembling heart," who wander up and down the earth, "outcasts from Zion's hallowed ground," we see that God remembers national sin:

> *Their glory faded and their race dispersed,*
> *The last of nations now, though once the first;*
> *They warn and teach the proudest, would they learn,*
> *Keep wisdom, or meet judgment in your turn.*
> *If we escaped not – if heaven spared not us–*
> *Peeled, scattered, and exterminated thus–*
> *If vice received her retribution due,*
> *When we were visited – what hope for you,*
> *When God arises with an awful frown,*
> *To punish lust, or pluck presumption down?*
> *When gifts perverted, or not duly prized,*
> *Pleasure o'ervalued, and His grace despised,*
> *Provoke the vengeance of His righteous hand,*
> *To pour down wrath upon a thankless land;*
> *He will be found impartially severe,*
> *Too just to wink or speak the guilty clear.*

The times in which we live appeal pre-eminently to our patriotism, and there is no virtue for the promotion and exercise of which Scripture gives more full directions than for this. And one of its primary principles is that which we have been now considering. If national sin brings with it national calamity, then the lengthening out of our prosperity must depend on the caution which is exercised lest any sin should be permitted and indulged, until it shall become distinctive of our national character. This is the first claim of Scriptural patriotism, and should it have so occurred – through the positive disregard of God's laws on the part of some, and through carelessness and indifference on the part of others, in not lifting up the voice of remonstrance against the sinful habits of their fellow-countrymen – that national sins have been contracted, then a Christian patriotism will manifest itself in deep humiliation on account of such neglect, in making a stand for God against the continuance of evil, and in reiterating that sentiment which of old was tendered to a proud monarch, who disregarded it, but to his cost: "Wherefore, let my counsel be acceptable unto thee, and break off thy sins by righteousness; if it may be a lengthening of thy tranquillity." (*Daniel 4:27*). Is there not a call for such an exercise of patriotism now?

Is there nothing in our religious condition as a people that demands it? Is there nothing among ourselves over which there floats, audible to the men who seek the best welfare of their country and deprecate its woe, the sound of that sentence, "I remember"? Are not its murmurs to be heard at this moment, amid political excitements and difficulties of administration? "I remember" the Sabbaths which are systematically broken by those who take their pleasure on my holy day. "I remember" the intemperance of those who "rise up early in the morning that they may follow strong drink; that continue until night, till wine inflame them." "I remember" the cupidity of those "who join house to house, and field to field;" where "I looked for judgment, but behold oppression," the cry of the widow passing for nothing, and the appeal for right snuffed at because it was the appeal of weakness. "I remember" the want of truthfulness in the manner of conducting business, the unjust advantages taken of the buyer, the false representations made by the seller, although my word has declared that "a false balance is abomination to the Lord, but a just weight is His delight." "I remember" the fearful immorality which hid not itself from public gaze, when "the daughters of the people walked with stretched forth necks and wanton eyes, walking and mincing as they went;" and not less do "I remember" the concealed iniquity of men who, with a fancied impunity, perpetrated the foulest crimes, reckless of every consideration but that of inconvenient exposure. "I remember" the formalism which, under the name of religion, taught men that rites could save them, and which went up and down among the towns and villages of the land, in which the Bible had preceded them with the message that Jesus Christ's blood was the only atonement, that Jesus Christ's priesthood afforded the only available intercession, and that the Holy Ghost was the exclusive source of real regeneration – went up and down to serve the cause of antichrist, by affirming that tradition was the rightful point of appeal for the soul that was anxious for light on questions of religious doctrine and practice, and that sacraments undoubtedly secured ultimate salvation, and produced present renewal of the heart.

And why, in our case, should this remembrance of national sins be regarded otherwise than as conveying the warning of national punishment, and as associated with the threatening of national visitation? Our patriotism, to be effective, must be of the right stamp; and to prove itself of this stamp it must itself consent to learn its lessons from that chief source of all instruction – the Scriptures – confirmed, as the sacred teachings are, by the dispensations of Divine Providence. But would it not be rebelling against the God of the Bible, and refusing to receive His counsel, if, with the instances before us of national sin followed by national punishment which have suggested these thoughts, we should, instead of taking heed to the matter as concerns our own country, give way to a cool insensibility, or smile incredulously at the idea of alarm, as being preposterously unnecessary and positively quite beside the mark.

What will conduce to the well-being of our country? is the question which at this very juncture is upon a thousand lips, and avowedly occupying a thousand hearts. And many are the answers given, and many are the plans proposed; but be they what they may, however in themselves well-considered and promising (as it would be an act of injustice not to pronounce some of them to be), we can hope for no success independently of the principles which a patriotism founded on Scripture, and adhering to its instructions, must admit, and will be prepared to carry into practice. Other voices have spoken: let the Bible itself speak.

This blessed book will tell us at once that the sins of nations are *accumulations of the sins of individuals*. It is observable how, in the reproofs addressed to ancient Israel, as well as to other ancient nations, various distinct classes of the community are mentioned as contributing their quota to the full amount, to the complete measure of national iniquity – the rulers, the people, the prophets, the priests, the men, the women, the young, the old – there is a subdivision which gives to national sin not only a substantial aspect, but most certainly an individual bearing. "For the people turneth not unto Him that smiteth them, neither do they seek the Lord of hosts. Therefore the Lord will cut off from Israel head and tail, branch and rush, in one day. The ancient and honourable, he is the head; and the prophet that teacheth lies, he is the tail. For the leaders of this people cause them to err; and they that are led of them are destroyed. Therefore the Lord shall have no joy in their young men, neither shall have mercy on their fatherless and widows: for every one is an hypocrite and an evil-doer, and every mouth speaketh folly." (*Isaiah 9:13-17*). "Rise up, ye women that are at ease; hear my voice, ye careless daughters; give ear unto my speech ... Tremble, ye women that are at ease; be troubled, ye careless ones." (*Isaiah 32:9, 11*). "Behold, their ear is uncircumcised, and they cannot hearken: behold, the word of the Lord is unto them a reproach; they have no delight in it. Therefore I am full of the fury of the Lord; I am weary with holding in: I will pour it out upon the children abroad, and upon the assembly of young men together: for even the husband with the wife shall be taken, the aged with him that is full of days ... For from the least of them even unto the greatest of them every one is given to covetousness; and from the prophet even unto the priest every one dealeth falsely." (*Jeremiah 6:10, 11, 13*). "Seest thou not what they do in the cities of Judah and in the streets of Jerusalem? The children gather wood, and the fathers kindle the fire, and the women knead their dough, to make cakes to the queen of heaven, and to pour out drink-offerings unto other gods, that they may provoke me to anger." (*Jeremiah 7:17, 18*).

There may be a diversity in the manner in which individuals may have been guilty, in reference to the sum total of the public guilt. Some may have been the direct actors, and others may have been partakers in their sins, either by giving their sanction and encouragement to evil, or even by reaping actual profit and gain from the wrong-doing, or by refraining from lifting up, on all right occasions, the voice of faithful censure against it. Yet when all is put together, it will present a spectacle exactly corresponding to that which the weeping prophet drew when, in another passage, he showed the manner in which national sin is the accumulation of individual crime, and the product of individual guilt, acting and reacting. "Your iniquities have turned away these things, and your sins have withholden good things from you. For among my people are found wicked men: they lay wait, as he that setteth snares; they set a trap, they catch men. As a cage is full of birds, so are their houses full of deceit: therefore they are become great, and waxen rich. They are waxen fat, they shine: yea, they overpass the deeds of the wicked: they judge not the cause, the cause of the fatherless, yet they prosper; and the right of the needy do they not judge. Shall I not visit for these things? saith the Lord: shall not my soul be avenged on such a nation as this?" But then to give a climax to the whole, and to show that the guilt of those who commit the sin is shared by those who encourage it, and to indicate that to refrain from uplifting the voice of instruction and warning upon these points, by those who hold the sacred office, is a fearful enhancement, by a class of individuals, of national guilt, it is added – "A wonderful and horrible thing is committed in the land; the prophets prophesy falsely, and the priests bear rule by their means; and my people love to have it so: and what will ye do in the end thereof?" (*Jeremiah 5:25-31*). We have dwelt the longer on this point – a point sufficiently obvious to reason, but too much denied its appropriate influence over our habitual practice – because it constitutes the very basis of all that action which Christian patriotism will take in securing its ends and purposes. From all which has been stated it will follow:

1. That it is a duty constantly incumbent upon us, as members of the community, to enquire into our personal relation to that public criminality of which God says, "I remember it," and to make it the matter of our individual repentance and humiliation. It is a deeply affecting view of sin which breaks upon us here; it has a double criminality, first, as being the development of our own individual guilt, and then as going to make up the sum of national delinquency. Do we enough regard it thus? and would not the habit of thus viewing it, were it more generally practised, issue in a repentance more truly enlightened, more literally national, and more blessedly and sincerely so, too, than can ever be procured by formal decrees or by official proclamations? Not that we take objection against these, far from it; but the practice which we propose has this advantage – that we can set about it at once, that we need not wait till we are called upon by others to enter upon it. Is our patriotism leading us in this direction? Is ours the patriotism of the chamber of devotion? of self-communion? of self-enquiry? of close personal investigation, busy in proposing such questions as these – In what measure have *my* sins contributed to that iniquity which God remembers and condemns as belonging to the nation? Do I add to its Sabbath-breaking, to its cupidity, to its impurity, to its formality? If

personally, and through God's grace, these things cannot be described as committed by me, yet do I give any sanction to them in others? Do I protest against them? Do I exert my influence to lessen their amount? Do I refuse to enter on my list of friends the men who practise them? or do I, by any inconsistency, any failure in any other respect, allow them to think lightly of religion, and so remove a check which might otherwise be felt and admitted by them? Whenever or wherever lived there a man in whose bosom burnt a purer flame of patriotism than Daniel? Imitate him; mark that combination of which he himself gives an account, when he tells us how the angel Gabriel found him praying, and adds, "and confessing *my* sin and the *sin of my people* Israel, and presenting my supplication before the Lord my God for the holy mountain of my God." (*Daniel 9:20*). Surely, if there were a point of view in which, in the thoughts of penitence and the language of prayer, Daniel could associate *his sin* personally and individually with *the sin of the people* – if he felt that, deprecating the continuance of God's wrath against Israel, he must plead for personal forgiveness – it cannot be otherwise than appropriate and necessary for us to do the same, and to enquire into our relation to that public criminality, of which God says, "I remember it," and to make it the matter of our own penitence and confession.

2. The sins of nations, which call down wrath, being thus the accumulation of the sins of individuals, those will do most to prevent public calamity, to ensure national prosperity, and thus will do most for their country, who make a stand for God against that which would displease Him; who, in their own immediate spheres, seek, in dependence upon His grace, to yield to His authority, and to illustrate His religion; and who "let their light so shine before men, that they may see their good works, and glorify their Father which is in heaven." (*Matthew 5:16*).

Personal religion is the best patriotism. The fear of God pervading men's hearts is the surest provision against national calamity, because it is the opposite of national sin. What claim has that man to be regarded as sincerely feeling for his country's welfare, who, as far as his life and actions go, is continually adding to the amount of his country's sins? What is the value, in the sight of God, of a man's patriotism, if his daily example, followed out by any considerable number in a neighbourhood, would render society insupportable? if his tastes are gratified in haunts, in acts, and habits which demoralise others and debase himself, and against which the wrath of God is revealed from heaven? He is the true lover of his country who, believing that "sin is the reproach of any people," carefully, prayerfully, as a member of the community, sets his face against it, in order that, insofar as he is concerned, his country may not have that reproach to bear. He is the true lover of his country who, believing that it is "righteousness," a holy integrity, "which exalteth a people," makes conscience of holiness, in order that he may have a share in its exaltation. He is the true lover of his country who begins with the province of his own heart and life, and who desires to have it purged of all which might draw down that terrible notice of Divine wrath, "I remember;" who seeks to extend the same influences in his domestic relationships; and who then comes forth into public life with all that weight which a blameless conduct gives, with all that power which transparency of character imparts, with all that inspiration which holiness affords when God is associated with secular duties, when in the citizen of earth men see that they have before them a citizen of heaven, and when there is nothing which friends have to conceal, nor anything which oozes out in the half-suppressed murmurs of those who are listening to his political suggestions, to his commendation of public measures, or his criticisms of public men – "Physician, heal thyself;" while thou "promisest liberty," thou thyself art "the servant of corruption."

Go, then, and exercise your civil privileges, your social rights, in the fear of the God of nations. Set him at your right hand. Pray much! that if there be things which He remembers, as indeed there are, the punishment may be averted, and mercy granted. Pray much! that you may be preserved from adding, by personal guilt, to the amount of remembered national transgression. Pray much! this privilege all can use, this franchise all possess. Pray! and then act consistently with prayer.

Yet, oh! forget not that if God remembers individual sins as making up the amount of national crimes, he also remembers them as *personal offences against Himself,* as matters between Himself and you, deserving to be visited by Him in righteous judgment. What if God were to open His lips at this moment, and, particularising our personal sins of omission and of commission, to say over each of them, "I remember," and to deal with us concerning them as we have deserved? Where now would be our standing place? That He has not long before this done so, and that He has not said to the messenger of His wrath, as He said to Saul by His prophet, "Now go and destroy," is only to be attributed to His forbearance and long-suffering. But His forbearance is not forgetfulness. It is "salvation" to those who use it as space for repentance, and who, mourning their sin, turn from their iniquity; but this very long-suffering will be an appalling aggravation to the sin and to the woe of those who use it only to persist in that which they know to be grievous to God's spirit, and opposed to His will. Would to God that we thought more frequently, more deeply, that *God remembers,* for then we should feel that persistence in known sin, however carefully concealed, however stealthily managed, however preceded by the look-out, first this way and then that, as though there were not an eye above which sees all ways and at all times – then we should feel that persistence in sin is but treasuring up wrath against the day of wrath. With this sentence before us – "I remember," – there comes a solemn appeal to those who are called to watch for souls, as they who must one day give account. "Cry aloud, spare not; show my people their transgressions and the house of Jacob their sins." (*Isaiah 58:1*). But if they warn, it is to save. If, on the one hand, this book tells the impenitent sinner that God does remember sin, on the other it tells the penitent, the broken-hearted transgressor of a way of peace, a way of life already provided in which, approaching God, he may find promises such as these realised – "Their sins and their iniquities will I remember no more." (*Hebrews 8:12*). "I will blot out as a cloud their transgressions, and as a thick cloud their sins." God has remembered sin; and the stroke fell upon his well-beloved Son, our Surety, and now "there is no condemnation to those who are in Christ Jesus:" now for His sake God will not deal with us according to our sins, nor reward us according to our iniquities. Be this our plea, then; however accumulated our transgressions, however long the reserve of merited wrath, there is grace to help us, there is mercy equal to our utmost need, "Though your sins be as scarlet, they shall be white as snow; though red like crimson, they shall be as wool." (*Isaiah 1:18*). To this forgiving God let those turn who are conscious of never yet having sincerely sought pardon and reconciliation. Ah! would you but do this, how blest the hour, how memorable the day, at once of your repentance and your peace! the day on which, for the first time, you could look up at God without dread, and feel that sin, *your sin,* had been "put away." Let that period be "*now.*" Determine, in the strength of God, that it shall be so; and then go, and, in dependence on the same power, carry your solemn resolution into effect at the mercy-seat.

Chapter 8
True and False Repentance

"Then Saul said, I have sinned: yet honour me now, I pray thee, before the elders of my people, and before Israel, and turn again with me, that I may worship the Lord thy God."
(*1 Samuel 15:30*)

THERE is not a duty more incumbent upon those who would walk in the fear of God and have their hearts right with Him, than that of learning how to discriminate between that which is real in religion, and that which only bears the semblance of being right and consistent with the will of God. It is a woeful act to "call evil good," to "put darkness for light, and bitter for sweet;" for to make a mistake here is eminently to sin against one's own soul. Yet the danger of confounding appearances with realities, of mistaking the one for the other, is by no means inconsiderable. Regard for self may be made to wear the appearance of zeal for God; pride may veil itself beneath a covering of apparent humility; and where, from certain circumstances, it might be imagined that there was real repentance, there may yet be concealed its very opposite. To know, then, how to distinguish – to be able to form a right judgment, so as neither to be misled ourselves, nor to allow others to mislead their own souls – is an acquisition of the highest moment, and it is one for which the sacred Scriptures furnish us with abundant materials. They set the real before us with its distinctive marks, and the unreal with its discoverable defects; and enabling us thus to make ourselves acquainted with both, they prepare us to apply these criteria to our own cases, and to form our conclusions accordingly, under the guidance of that gracious Spirit who, if implored, will never fail to assist the diligent student of God's Word, in his effort to "compare spiritual things with spiritual."

Now were it the question with us, How may we discriminate between a *merely seeming* repentance and *genuine* penitence? there is hardly a passage of Scripture which could render us more decided assistance than that portion of Saul's history which here claims attention. It brings before us most vividly a certain number of circumstances, the presence of which is at once decisive against the existence of genuine contrition. That we may ascertain what these are, that we may carry them in our recollection, so as to apply them, is undoubtedly the reason for which we are put in possession of an inspired record of this particular part of that incident in the history of Saul which has already been under consideration. Its prayerful study will contribute to our scriptural acquisitions, and enlarge that power of spiritual discernment on which, under God, depends our spiritual safety. Apparently, Saul is penitent. He had wilfully disobeyed the commandment of God; the further opportunity afforded him of manifesting the spirit of reverence and regard for Him who had constituted him king over Israel had been lost. Samuel had spoken with a sternness which formed no part of his natural character, but which was becoming in the servant of the Most High God, when he rebuked the gross dishonour which had been done to His name. The vain excuses beneath which Saul had attempted to cover his sin had all been flung away by the arguments of the man of God. The sentence before uttered, that the kingdom should be taken away from him, had now been reiterated and solemnly confirmed. We look for the effect of all this on the guilty prince, and we hear him say, "I have sinned;" we hear him repeat it. And is not this repentance? What more can be required? Is it not enough that such an avowal should be made? "I have transgressed the commandment of the Lord and thy word." Has not the stern rebuke taken effect? Has not the solemn admonition penetrated his soul? Is not the result exactly that which was most to be desired? and is not the confession appropriate and well-expressed?

Besides, he desires immediately to engage in the worship of God. He cannot give this up. He would bow at the altar, and present the sacrifice. Moreover, he treats the servant of God with the greatest outward respect. He does not impugn the justice of the sentence. He appears to yield to it all; and instead of separating himself from God's minister, he is only anxious that Samuel should stay with him, and deprecates his turning away from him as a thing which he can hardly endure. Surely, we are ready to say, these manifestations are of the most favourable kind – Saul is a penitent!

It cannot, however, escape our observation that Samuel did not seem to think so. There was no notice taken of these confessions in the way of approval or sympathy. He turned away, firmly and decidedly. Yet Samuel, even to the last, had manifested so deep, so affectionate an interest in all that pertained to Saul's welfare, and had taken such pains to set him right and keep him right, that when we see him parting from him, and refusing to respond to these admissions of guilt, and to recognise the worship thus proposed, we are surprised at first; and we can only account for Samuel's manner on one ground, that he did not believe the king to be penitent at all – that he saw in him a man who was sorry, but not contrite, for his wrong-doing – mortified because he had *committed himself,* but not abhorring himself in dust and ashes because *he had grieved the Spirit of God.* Of course, if it were so, Samuel was amply justified in turning away as he did. To have done otherwise would have been to have countenanced Saul's hypocrisy, and to have added to his criminality; it would have been to have descended from that high position of ministerial fidelity which can never be tampered with except at the certainty of incurring the loss of God's favour and at the same time the secret contempt – however concealed under the apparently friendly regard – of those who have been conciliated by unfaithfulness, instead of being rebuked with unflinching truthfulness. The question for us is, therefore, do we discern anything in the manner or the matter of Saul's expressions which would lead to the suspicion that his contrition was not sincere, and that the avowed penitent was the real impenitent? And to that question the narrative furnishes a very distinct reply. For instance:

I. We see that though there was confession, it was not made until Saul was actually compelled to make it, because the evidence of his sin was incontrovertibly clear. The very rapidity with which he altered his tone was a proof that he acted under a pressure which it was absolutely impossible to resist. At first, he positively denied ever having done anything wrong in the matter. He said he was entirely innocent. "I have performed the commandment of the Lord;" there is nothing wrong. A piercing question from Samuel somewhat lowered his tone, and he made an approach to an admission that his regard to the divine commandment had not been so exact and accurate as it might have been; but then he excused himself by implying that he meant no harm. And now, when the prophet thoroughly exposes his sin, he who a few moments before declared his innocence, affirms, "I have sinned: for I have transgressed the commandment of the Lord, and thy words." We see that the confession is wrung from him inch by inch, and it only comes at last when, as far as the facts were concerned, it made no difference whether he confessed or not, for he was proved to be guilty. We discover at once, in this circumstance, the opposite of that state of mind which feels the weight of personal sin, and which longs to unburden itself; and, as we compare it with that Scripture, (*Proverbs 28:13*), which says, "He that covereth his sins shall not prosper: but whoso confesseth and forsaketh them shall have mercy," we are compelled to regard Saul's action rather as a bungling attempt to cover his sin – an attempt which, after all, did not succeed – than as that unburdening of conscious guilt which is alone consistent with true penitence.

II. A second proof against Saul's real penitence is his attempt to palliate the crime which he had confessed, by throwing the blame on other persons – "The people took of the spoil." According to his own view, he was more to be pitied than blamed – "I feared the people, and obeyed their voice." They were the tempters, according to his representation, but for whom he would never have thought of straying from the paths of obedience. But even were it so, his conduct could not be extenuated by such a consideration. It was his duty, not only not to have listened for a moment to their voice, but to have set them, without hesitation, an example of decided and uncorrupted holiness. His position demanded it, and rendered it easy too. A word from him, supposing that they were the tempters and he the tempted, would have shown them the uselessness of their efforts to turn him from the path of duty. It was his to resist, to rise superior to their proposal, and not to pander to their corruption.

The sacred narrative, however, distinctly affirms that this sin was as much his act and deed as the people's; nor is it likely that it would have been done by them except it had been proposed by him. There was, therefore, a want of justice in this attempt at extenuation. But it is not thus that we find those acting, who are set before us in Scripture as examples of true repentance. There is no attempt to palliate when David, in *Psalm 51*, sues for mercy; nay, he admits to the full his transgression. *His* desire is that "God may be justified when He speaks" in accusation, and "be clear when He judges." His confession goes deeper than to the commission of the crime; it extends to the humbling acknowledgment of a guilty and corrupt nature, as the source to which his sin was traceable, and over which he mourns. "Behold, I was shapen in iniquity, and in sin did my mother conceive me." And nothing short of this will ever prove that the spirit is truly contrite, that the heart is really broken – nothing but the full, the unrestricted confession, "I acknowledged my sin unto Thee, and mine iniquity have I not hid. I said, I will confess my transgressions to the Lord; and thou forgavest the iniquity of my sin." (*Psalm 32:5*).

III. A third proof against Saul was his greater anxiety to have the forgiveness of Samuel than to receive the pardon of God – the prominent place he gave to the one above the other consideration, "Now therefore, I pray thee, pardon my sin, and turn again with me, that I may worship the Lord." Surely, if there had been a genuine view of his sinfulness, as committed against God, when he uttered the sentence, "I have transgressed the commandment of the Lord, and thy words," he would have first and directly gone to the Lord for pardon, for there was no comparison between the two cases, as to the guilt implied in each. Certainly, it was trifling with the solemn office which Samuel held, and not less trifling with all the kind and tender interest which the prophet had ever manifested towards him as a friend, when Saul recklessly left his message unfulfilled, except as far as agreed with his own interest or convenience. It was an offence, a grave offence, against God's servant, a wanton insult, a purchasing of his own gratification at the expense of every tender and sacred feeling for one whose advice he had often received, and in whose prayers he had largely participated. There was, indeed, good ground on which he might ask to have been forgiven by his friend. But the main feature of his sin was its flagrant violation of *the law of God;* its direct and unmitigated opposition to His will; his preference for his own sordid purposes above the will – the strongly expressed will – of God. This was the primary view to be taken of his guilt; and had it been taken by himself, not a moment would have been lost in seeking that forgiveness from God which he now seemed only anxious to obtain from man. What argued that postponement of God's pardon till he was reconciled to man – what but that he treated it as a matter which did not press immediately, which could be arranged subsequently? Could any real mourner for sin have felt thus? with such a penitent, is not the thought of God the one exciting, all-pervading idea in his contrition? – God, as sinned against – God, as the sole source of pardon – God, as able and willing to forgive? The thought that sin has been committed against such a God – so great, so good, so long-suffering – is that which gives poignancy to the wounds of conscience. Its effect is to throw into the shade, for the time, all other considerations. David had sinned against man as well as against God. The broken heart of Uriah, and then his murder – the dishonour of Bathsheba – never surely was there more of sin against man mixed up with offence against God; and yet, when David poured out his penitential feelings at the footstool of mercy, there were moments, when the view of his sin as against God so completely absorbed and engrossed his mind, as to exclude for the time all other views, all other associations; and when the cry that arose from his lips told how thoroughly he was overpowered by the remembrance, "Against thee, thee *only* have I sinned, and done this evil in thy sight." And only by the pardon of God is such a state of mind met. In vain may man utter sounds of reconciliation and words of forgiveness; the language of the penitent, as he remembers against whom he has offended, and whose displeasure he has incurred, will be:

"No voice but Thine can give me rest."

"Have mercy upon me, O God, according to thy loving-kindness, according to the multitude of thy tender mercies blot out my transgressions." How strange the contrast presented by the case before us, to that view of sincere repentance of which the Psalmist was the subject! There was fervour, indeed, in Saul, but fervour in the wrong direction. He would press his point with the prophet, and gain forgiveness if he could, but Samuel "turned about to go away." He could not sanction that which he felt was a fresh dishonour to God; and as he turned away, the miserable king laid hold of the skirt of his garment, and it rent – a circumstance which, while it showed the intensity of his desire to gain Samuel's friendly notice, and the determination, on the other hand, of the prophet not to bestow it, served also as a type of the penalty which God affixed to his rebellion: "And Samuel said, The Lord hath rent the kingdom of Israel from thee this day, and hath given it to a neighbour of thine, that is better than thou. And also the Strength of Israel will not lie nor repent: for He is not a man, that He should repent." (*1 Samuel 15:28, 29*).

It might have been thought that such a denunciation as this would have aroused within Saul's bosom a higher and more correct order of feelings; that it would have brought his sin before him in such a form as to divert his mind from his pursuit of man's favourable regard as a primary object, and that thus it would have contributed to a more hopeful manifestation of repentance. But no; it did not stir him from his lethargy, nor drive him from his mistake. It only brought out more fully the real object which he had in view in being so anxious for Samuel's forgiveness.

IV. There is a fourth circumstance which throws suspicion on the penitence of Saul – the manner in which he showed that all his desire was to stand well in public estimation, notwithstanding that it was an undoubted fact that he had publicly sinned, and incurred the divine displeasure. He had evidently forfeited his claim on the good opinion of those around him. In the case of a man for whom God had done so much, but who had so notoriously ill-requited the favours shown him – a man whose position demanded that he should be an example of all that was obedient and deferential to God, but who had himself thus wantonly rebelled against Him whose glory it should have been his first object to promote – it was to be expected that, having lost the favour of God, he would lose the regard of those around him. In whatever degree the fear and love of God prevailed among the people of Israel, in that same degree would Saul sink in popular estimation. Every right-minded Israelite would condemn him; would pity him, indeed, but would find it impossible to think well of him. So it should ever be; those who despise God must expect to be lightly esteemed. Before it could be otherwise in any community, there must be a grievous blunting of their moral feelings, a melancholy deterioration in their moral standard. And against this deterioration, this want of moral sensitiveness, communities do well to guard. That must be an evil state of things which would enable a wrong-doer to obtain from public opinion an award in his favour; and what must have become of the cause of integrity – of honour – of justice – of all that is excellent, where, by reason of the low state of moral feeling, the voice of society is no longer heard to pronounce its verdict, distinctly and emphatically, against evil-doers and in praise of those who do well. In this respect, every community incurs a deep responsibility. Society constitutes a jury always sitting; bound to be faithful to the King of kings, and to return a true verdict on individual character and conduct, and it is at their peril that they are partial. Charitable they ought to be; ready to put the best construction on all that is doubtful, receiving as fact nothing which is not fully proved; but to justify the evil-doer, to give him a favourable verdict, to admit him to the privileges of regard, and respect, and friendship, as though he were not a wrong-doer – this is as great a wrong as if, in a court of justice, a jury were to acquit the offender whose guilt could not be doubted, and it must issue in the same evil results, of bringing contempt on the law, and of encouraging instead of repressing sin.

Thoughts such as these find a response in our moral nature, and hence the legitimate desire to receive a favourable award from the society in which we move – a desire which, under God, is largely and beneficially operative as a check upon sin. But still, to a rightly constituted mind, even the favourable verdict of public opinion would be of little worth, except as it echoed the verdict of the court of heaven. That is the highest acquisition, "favour *with God* and man;" but the latter always in subordination to the former, never as a substitute for it. With too many, alas! the case is exactly the reverse. If they can but be well received in society, if they can but pass in the court of popular opinion, they look no higher. They forget that there is a superior tribunal to which not only they themselves, but those who have tried them, are amenable. They ask not for God's concurrent testimony, nor trouble themselves about it. There is even a still more awful case than this, and it occurs when men, knowing that the judgment of God is against them, that the sentence of God condemns them, and having reason to fear that the judgment of man will be against them too, bend all their energies to secure a favourable award from man, as a counterbalance to that which conscience tells them God has pronounced. They cannot blind their eyes or close their ears to the state of things between God and their own souls, but they seek a set-off against it in such a treatment at the hands of their fellow-men as would indicate that they had not lost caste by their criminality. And this was the part which Saul acted. Hear it in his own words: "I have sinned: yet honour me now, I pray thee, before the elders of my people, and before Israel, and turn again with me, that I may worship the Lord thy God." Behold the man who had just heard God's opinion of himself from God's own messenger! He fears that the next step will be the marked displeasure of the people. But if he can avert that, if he can keep them in good humour with himself, if he can secure their recognition, if he can induce them to treat him as though nothing were the matter, why then he can afford to bear the removal of God's favour. And what is his plan in order to accomplish this end? It is two-fold. First, he will appear religious; he will stand before the people as a worshipper of the Lord. He will pay the outward sacrifice, and offer the external service. That nothing more than what was external is meant here is quite evident from the fact that he referred to God merely as being the object of His creatures' homage, and that even when he thus mentioned Him, it was in a manner most cold and distant, a manner which no man who had a spark of right feeling towards an offended God, or of proper feeling about himself as the offender, would have adopted – "That I may worship the Lord *thy* God." *Thy* God! Could a true penitent have been satisfied thus to have designated that God who had been everything to him, and who alone, if pardon was ever obtained, must dispense it? and did not the expression exactly agree with a selfish and formal religion, intended only to be seen of men? But Saul reckoned that the people would think the better of him if he still ranked among the worshippers of God; he knew that to have given this up would have told effectually against him. There was something even beyond this. He knew that very much of the success of any effort which he might make to keep his place in the good opinion of the community would depend upon the way in which he was treated by Samuel. If the venerable prophet refused to be his companion and his friend, then it was to be apprehended that his position would be materially damaged. "Honour me now before the people," therefore, became Saul's cry. "Do not let them see that you do not think well of me. Treat me as you have ever treated me. Pay me respect before them." Here we see why it was that Saul was so anxious to have Samuel's forgiveness. Even here, his predominant selfishness comes out to view. Samuel knew this; for the man who does not care about God's forgiveness can have no proper motive for caring about his fellow-creatures' pardon. It was selfishness, after all; and can we – dare we – dignify with the name of penitence this poor contrivance for patching up a broken reputation, by seeking from man's favour what might be a substitute for the loss of divine approval?

We blame not Saul for being anxious about public esteem, but we do blame him for being more solicitous about this than about God's judgment. We blame him for seeking it, too, on such grounds as those which prompted him, and by such means as those which he employed – by formality towards God whom he virtually renounced – by currying favour with a man who was bound to be faithful to the God of truth, whoever was offended by his fidelity. Ah, wretched man! thou hadst already sunk in public estimation, thou hadst lost ground; but painful as was thy position, there were better and more noble means of recovery than those which thou didst use. Hadst thou but humbled thyself before God – hadst thou but sought and found from Him another heart – hadst thou confessed with genuineness thy wrong-doing, and made no efforts (vain as they were) to cover it – hadst thou altered in thy life, and caused it to be seen as evidently that thou couldst no more trifle with God's commands, as it had been evident to all that thou hadst sinned and gone astray – hadst thou, with an outward regard to religion, combined its secret exercises, and chosen the path of retirement, in order to "mourn apart" and let wounds of conscience bleed, to be bound up only by a heavenly hand – why then thou, even thou, wouldst have known how God exalts those who humble themselves under His mighty hand, and then thou mightest have experienced, what many have found, that even the court of human opinion is not unrelenting against the man upon whom an unfavourable verdict has once been pronounced, but who gives proofs of sincere contrition – that a broken reputation is not irreparable – and that no way to the recovered favour even of man is surer than a course of retired and consistent humiliation before God. Where God forgives, His church will not be slow to recognise His act; and with all its uncharitableness, there is candour and kindness enough yet in the world to restore to its good opinion the man who, while he seeks this restoration, proves his sorrow for the past in conduct characterised by frank avowal, meekness, and humbleness of mind, by decided giving up of what has been wrong, and by a manifest effort to repair the wrong of which he has been guilty.

The narrative tells us that Samuel turned at length, when Saul asked him, but not to sanction his sin – turned, but not to make himself a party to Saul's hypocrisy. He waited but to give one public testimony to God; to take advantage of Saul's disobedience to show, in a manner never to be forgotten – to illustrate, in the slaughter of Agag by his own hand, that what God commands must be done, at whatever cost of private feeling: and then we read, in words the pathetic force of which it would be impossible to enhance, though quite possible to diminish, by a single syllable of enlargement – words, the suggestiveness of which is sufficiently clear as to our own duty, as professing Christians, towards public offenders against the commands of God who have, time after time, been warned, but who still persist in sin – "Then Samuel went to Ramah; and Saul went up to his house, to Gibeah of Saul. And Samuel came no more to see Saul until the day of his death: nevertheless, Samuel mourned for Saul." (*1 Samuel 15:34, 35*).

Such is one of the most affecting contributions which Scripture supplies towards enabling us to judge between sincere contrition and that false repentance which, after all, is actual, downright impenitence. So loud is the call for repentance, so impossible is it to obtain pardon without it, so certain that there can be no real faith in the divine way of pardon which is not accompanied by real penitence, that no care can be too great, no caution too constant, in enquiring into the nature of our own personal repentance. The assurance that God will not reject the truly contrite is decidedly another reason for diligent self-enquiry. Let Saul's conduct teach us what we have to avoid, what we must be dissatisfied with, what, if we have done the like, needs first and immediately itself to be repented of. "Take with you words and return to the Lord;" the words He Himself has given, the feelings appropriate to those words He waits to bestow.

That penitential psalm, to which we have before adverted, we still commend. Take it – use it – pray it. Yes, pray it as your own prayer, and offer it as your own petition. "Purge me with hyssop, and I shall be clean: wash me, and I shall be whiter than snow ... Hide thy face from my sins, and blot out all mine iniquities. Create in me a clean heart, O God; and renew a right spirit within me. Cast me not away from thy presence; and take not thy holy spirit from me. Restore unto me the joy of thy salvation." (*Psalm 51:7, 9-12*).

And not in vain shall this prayer be offered, for listen to that most gracious promise, "Thus saith the Lord, The heaven is my throne, and the earth is my footstool ... but to this man will I look, even to him that is poor and of a contrite spirit, and trembleth at my word." (*Isaiah 66:1, 2*). Not in vain shall this prayer be offered, for is it not written, "Let the wicked forsake his way, and the unrighteous man his thoughts: and let him return unto the Lord, and He will have mercy upon him; and to our God, for He will abundantly pardon"? (*Isaiah 55:7*). Oh! who would resist the call, or delay and hold back? What pleasure in sin, what gratification in a fancied independence of religious control, or in a vaunted high-spiritedness which will not stoop to take spiritual advice, can for a moment be compared with the joy of pardoned guilt – the joy of hearing the Spirit's witness to pardon sealed, "Thy sins be forgiven thee; go in peace"?

Chapter 9
Playing the Fool

"Behold, I have played the fool, and have erred exceedingly."
(*1 Samuel 26:21*)

HOW wonderful is the effect of a single flash of lightning, when previously the heavens had been veiled in deepest gloom, and the darksome night had thrown over all nature its dreariest mantle. How completely, for a moment, it lifts that mantle up. How suddenly and peremptorily it throws that veil aside. How distinctly you see the whole of what had been erewhile concealed. Houses, trees, streets, public edifices – they burst upon you; you seem never to have seen them so distinctly before. You recognise them, but there is at the same time a startling freshness about them, which thrills through you as you gaze. And yet it is but for a moment; while you look, the flash is gone. It appeared to have come from behind those clouds whose lights and shadows, in its transient glare, reminded you of some vast mountain ridge seen at a distance; and there, among them, it disappeared. It lasted long enough to make you feel its effect, and then it departed. How different from such a spectacle is the first gleam of day which pierces the shades of night, and announces the dawn. It is not so brilliant; its discoveries are not so vivid at first; but it makes progress; and as line after line of dark cloud recedes, till at length there is perfect day, you have a view of the objects around you, complete as that which the lightning-flash had imparted, and yet far preferable, because it is permanent. "I have played the fool, and have erred exceedingly," – it tells of such a sudden gleam. To our view, in a moment it lays open the whole features of Saul's history, as he saw them himself. From beginning to end, his eye is fixed upon all that had transpired from the moment at which the crown was placed on his brow until the period at which he now stood, not far from his end, in circumstances of most pitiable humiliation. Nothing escapes him; each avenue opens up its concealment, each pathway reveals the footsteps imprinted along it; and there is nothing which is satisfactory, nothing which is not condemnatory. What fatal errors has he committed; what grievous wrongs has he inflicted on himself and others; "played the fool – erred exceedingly," – and then the gloom returned, the deeper darkness which never was succeeded by the day of light and peace. It was not the dawn of true repentance, gradually unfolding reason for encouragement, notwithstanding deep consciousness of demerit, and losing itself in brighter hopes and lasting joy; but it was the sudden flash which conscience, when excited, will send through a soul, preliminary only to a deeper despair – to hopeless ruin.

But ah! to be, as Saul now was, drawing fast to the close of life with such a sentence as this on his lips! It was not the state of things which would have been anticipated on that day on which he began his public life, appointed by God Himself to fill the throne of Israel. Yet who shall tell how many, besides this unhappy prince, have been constrained to use these very words of their own cases, to look upon their courses in the self-same light – many who little expected it once for themselves, of whom once it would scarcely have been anticipated by others. By no means singular then, this exclamation of Saul presents to us a solemn warning; and that we may escape that dreary conclusion at which he was forced to arrive, let us survey, with prayerful attention and faithful self-enquiry, the circumstances which gave rise to and mournfully justified this melancholy utterance, and learn what those courses are which, transferred to our own cases and illustrated in our own histories, would be our folly – our exceeding great error.

I. We may notice, generally, that Saul's history justifies this expression, inasmuch as his public life was marked by a continued attempt at thorough independence of God. Here is discoverable the great secret of Saul's downfall. This was his folly, here he erred. Where God's requirements fell in with his convenience, called for no self-denial, and did not interfere at all with self-will, he performed them. But when these divine commands contravened his inclinations, crossed his purposes, interrupted his gratifications, touched his pride, and made him feel that God had the right to control, then his whole conduct showed a determination to have his own way, and you could read in his procedures that the principle of his life was, "I will do as I like – I will have things my own way – I will not be controlled – I will not be dictated to." Up to a certain point there was sometimes an expressed deference, but whenever he chose to transgress a command, which he did whenever it proved inconvenient to his high and independent spirit, he did not hesitate to offend God. And then, when God rebuked him, he did not reform; and when God forsook him, he deliberately made the attempt, instead of going back to God in humiliation – he made the attempt to get on without God.

This was folly – first, because *it was subversive of all that reason and wisdom suggested.* For the very being of a God is of itself a fact sufficiently indicative of the place which the creatures of that God should occupy. It was attempting to alter the relative positions of the Universal Sovereign and of His subjects – the relative position of the Great Proprietor of all and of those who are entirely at His disposal – the relative position of the Great Parent of all and of the members of His family. The laws of nature, in regard to matter, allow no interference with them which would subvert the relative conditions of strength and weakness, independence and dependence, without such results as expose the folly of the attempt. Let the lighter materials, of which the superstructure may be safely built, be employed for the foundation, and let the heavy blocks – the solid masses – of which the foundation should consist, be used for the superstructure, and the builder will soon have to say, "I have played the fool, and have erred exceedingly." Attempt to frame a raft of some substance whose specific gravity is greater than that of water, and the moment you launch it on the waves it will sink, and imminent peril will ensue, and you will just have been "playing the fool." Or come to nature's laws as regards moral beings – indulge a course of action which subverts these. Let the rule be that the child's will shall take precedence of the parent's, the servant's of the master's, that superior and inferior should change places, and would not the results in families and households soon prove that all this was but "erring exceedingly"? And on the same principle must there be read out the condemnation of downright folly when man so acts as to take upon himself the right to dictate for his own guidance, where God has uttered His voice – to make selections from God's will, and say what portion he will obey and which part he will disown. What is this but an attempt to subvert that which is fixed irrevocably? what but for man to turn aside from his proper place, and try to be a God himself? – an enterprise which can never succeed. No! let the tall mountain be turned upside down, let the narrow peak which crowns it take the position of its wide-spread base – will it stand? No! let the hand dispute the mastery with the head – can it take its place or discharge its functions? No! let the branch rebel against the stout old tree – can it bear the same weight or weather the same storms?

Choose what you will to illustrate the idea of strange and wilful subversion of appointed arrangements, and you see the folly – because you see the fruitlessness – of the case. And shall there be any success where man, dependent man, thus takes or attempts to take the place of independence? Can he rid himself of God, when, at the utmost stretch of self-will, he is asking, "Who is Lord over me?"

Besides, secondly, if it be against all reason to put our own will into the place of God's, *it is not less against our interest* to do so. Saul, indeed, attempted to do as well without God as with Him; but did he succeed? It may be said that a measure of prosperity attended some of his enterprises: but we ask, Did he gain enjoyment even from these? was he the happier for them? Does he not present to us the picture of a man continually ill at ease with himself and everyone around him – restless, unhappy even on the throne? And looking onwards to the state of the kingdom when death snatched it from his hands, we see that it had never realised the hopes which might have been entertained concerning it, from such an auspicious entrance upon its administration as was allotted to Saul. Did he get on as well without God as with Him? And did ever the history of a single individual justify the supposition that this was possible? We do not mean to say that there are not instances in which, where there is impiety in the heart and a proud defiance of the restrictions of true religion, there is permitted the attainment of earthly desires, or the acquisition of favourite secular objects; but where these come without a blessing, they, in a manner which their possessors can but ill conceal, afford no real comfort, and minister nothing to positive enjoyment. It is only "the blessing of the Lord" which "maketh rich, and He addeth no sorrow with it."

But there are cases innumerable, in which you see men continually interrupted in the prosecution of their aims and purposes. They scarcely ever seem to make way; and if they have prosperity in any degree, it never lasts long. It is like the case of Saul with the Philistines, a perpetual struggle with something that seems opposite and antagonistic; victory occasionally declaring for them, but the respite is small, for there is sure to be some Philistine soon again at their gates. And they are restless and uneasy. Like Saul, they have no comfort in their homes, though there be much, even to the possession of some lovely Jonathan, to calm and tranquillise their spirits; and, like him, they minister discomfort around them, ever keeping some javelin at hand to fling, if all is not exactly to their mind. You may wonder at what you see, but it is a distinct effect clearly traceable to a simple cause. They are trying to get on without God's blessing. They are attempting cross purposes with Him. They are at variance with Him, and they will not give in. The Lord is having a controversy with them, just because they will not be childlike and obedient. Surely they are their own enemies. Such a course cannot end well. They may not perceive it now, but they will some day. These are the things which pave the way for a review like that which, as it is described by the lips of the unhappy subject of our study, makes us tremble: "I have played the fool, and have erred exceedingly." We look on and tremble; and the language of the prophet becomes appropriate: "Lord, when thine hand is lifted up, they will not see; *but they shall see.*"

II. There was one particular course of action which was, at the moment at which Saul uttered these words, more especially present to his view; and, applicable as the sentence was to the whole retrospect of his history, it was pre-eminently appropriate to this portion of it. In many respects he had thus erred; in one respect most especially and distressingly so.

He was now addressing David, a man whom, on every ground, he ought to have loved, for he was lovely in himself, and he had done Saul good service; and, moreover, he stood in very near relationship to him – the husband of his daughter, the bosom-friend of his son. The circumstances under which David and himself were originally brought together were calculated to have produced, on the part of Saul, a lasting and an affectionate regard to David. From the moment that Samuel left him, after he had pronounced upon him the divine judgment, a deep-seated melancholy took possession of his mind, the immediate result of the agency of one of those evil spirits who have a power, though they cannot use it without divine permission, to produce physical discomfort as well as spiritual detriment. In this case, the permission was given by God, in the exercise of His judicial displeasure. According to Scripture phraseology, which assigns to God, not simply what He does directly, but what He permits, it is called "an evil spirit from the Lord." But before the sweet melody of David's harp Saul's melancholy gave way; his depression left him; his spirit was "refreshed and he was well:" and this sense of relief for a while led to the cherishing of affectionate feelings on the part of the king towards the skilful player.

When but a youth, the least of all his father's house, anointing oil poured upon David's head had marked him for some high and distinguished purpose, though there is no evidence to show that Saul was acquainted with the divine intention until a later period; and when still a stripling, he had relieved Saul and his army from the perplexity into which they had been thrown by the boastful defiance and the high-toned challenge of Goliath and the Philistines. That such an act should have been welcome to the subjects of Saul was only natural; and that the women out of the cities of Judah should sing, "Saul hath slain his thousands, but David his tens of thousands." They did this in the fulness of their hearts; and the last thing in their thoughts was that Saul would be offended by it. It was so true, that they thought Saul would of course admit it; and it was so joyous, that they thought that no one would be more gratified by hearing it than the king who had profited so largely by the prowess which the young man had shown. But they gave the proud and selfish king credit for what he did not possess. A generous mind would have joined in the chorus, and felt a satisfaction in doing so; but from the bosom of Saul whatever excellences of character he once possessed were fast declining now. "And Saul eyed David from that day and forward." A deep-rooted jealousy had taken possession of his soul; and it may serve to show how fast some weeds of corruption will spring up and gain maturity, and what a favourable soil for such a growth the heart of man presents, when forsaken by God – to notice, that by the time the morrow's sun had risen, after the day on which Saul first heard the gladsome songs of the daughters of Israel, he was ready and prepared to slay David. The evil spirit gained advantage from his state of mind; its influence was not now to be charmed away. The harp of David – which had cheered him when he was depressed, which had possessed the power to drive away his melancholy heretofore – was powerless now that his jealousy was aroused; and notwithstanding that he played as at other times, and the music was as touching, and the melody as sweet, Saul's mad and murderous scream, "I'll smite him to the wall," rose shrill above those tuneful notes, and the javelin in a moment left his hand, allowing the object of his malignity scarcely time to make his escape. That act of attempted murder was but the first of a series of efforts to bring about the death of David. When means direct proved unavailing, more secret methods were adopted; until at length, to save his life, the persecuted son of Jesse was compelled to wander hither and thither, deprived of the comforts of home – the mountain-fastness his refuge by day, and the cave in the side of the rock his shelter by night. It would appear that at length the infatuated king of Israel became alive to the fact that David was destined to be his successor on the throne – that it was, indeed, to him that Samuel alluded upon that occasion on which he had said, as he reproved Saul, "But now thy kingdom shall not continue: the Lord hath sought him a man after His own heart, and the Lord hath commanded him to be captain over His people, because thou hast not kept that which the Lord commanded thee." (*1 Samuel 13:14*). He saw, too, the public attention riveted on David; and thus he felt that a fresh confirmation was given to the prospect that the object of his hatred would be the next to wear the crown. Time after time he summoned his followers to hunt down his intended victim; and once and again, when he was really in the power of the man whose life he sought, David, with a forbearance which was as magnanimous in its aspect as it was truly pious in the motives from which it sprung, refused to retaliate, and Saul was allowed to escape. It was on the last of these occasions that the king of Israel gave utterance to the confession of his lamentable folly. Among the rocks of Engedi, David might have slain him, but he did not; and when Saul discovered that he owed his life to the forbearance of the man whom he was pursuing, his heart was touched, and bursting into tears, he commended David's act of mercy towards himself, at the same time acquiescing in his succession to the throne. But this right state of mind had not been permanent; and now, in the wilderness of Ziph, he again appeared scouring the country at the head of three thousand chosen men. After a day thus spent, at dead of night deep sleep had fallen on him and his band, when David and his attendant came so near that they took the spear from his bolster and the cruse of water from his side. He awoke to find again that he owed his life to David, and then it was that, touched by this new proof of the real feelings with which he was regarded by the object of his vindictive persecution, his thoughts went back to the whole course of treatment which David had received at his hand, and he said, "I have played the fool, and have erred exceedingly." It is not difficult to gather the reasons of this verdict pronounced upon himself; and they demand our attention, because they expose to our view points of possible error in our own conduct.

1. His folly and error consisted in treating a man as his enemy who was, in reality, his best friend. Judging from what David had done for Saul, it is easy to conceive the amount of service which he might have rendered him, had he been allowed to remain in peace, and had the opportunity been afforded him of directing his energies to the matters of the kingdom. If ever there was a man who stood in need of a friend in whom he could confide, and on whom he could devolve his cares, that man was Saul; and if there was one person above another in Israel able and willing to live and labour, to act and serve on behalf of the king, that individual was David. There was a beautiful manliness about his character; there was a peculiar disinterestedness in his soul; there was a courage which was never daunted, and a patriotism which shone brightly amid special difficulties. And you never see David attempting to supplant Saul in the affections of the people. He is never the rival – always the subject. He makes not the slightest approach to that sneaking meanness and to those low arts which, in after times, stamped with so much hatefulness the character of his own son, Absalom, when he set up as rival of his father; when, sitting in the gate, he courted popularity by telling any applicant for judgment that his cause was unquestionably good, that the king was indolent and indifferent, that if only he were "judge in the land" all

would be right; and then, to serve his own purpose, put forth his hand, and grasped and embraced with an unseemly familiarity the very persons whom, at any other time, and under any other circumstances, he would have passed with a haughty stare, and pretended not to know them. But no such pandering to wrong feelings marked the conduct of David to Saul, as that which characterised Absalom's conduct to David. He was a reliable man; and he showed it to the last. And at the moment referred to in the passage we are now studying, this truth appeared to flash upon the mind of Saul: "Here, for month after month, and year after year, have I been treating as an enemy a man who really is attached to me; who respects my life; who stands between me and those who would harm me! How happy might I have been with him at my side! How relieved might I have been with him in my councils! But all this advantage I have lost. 'I have played the fool, and have erred exceedingly.'" And when he recollected that such an one as Doeg the Edomite – a base, low-minded fellow – had been allowed to stand in his presence, to court his favour, to tell him tales, and help him in his misdeeds, it must have been with a pang that he remembered how he had treated David.

In this false, selfish world, and continually exposed as we are to evil from our own personal imperfections, God cannot give us a greater earthly blessing than *a real friend* – one who will be to us all that David would have been to Saul – one who will make our interests his own, who will lose himself in us, and whose presence and whose kindliness, like the harp of David, will cheer us when we become depressed, and restore us, when our thoughts and feelings will perversely flow in a direction contrary to our peace. And such a friend being brought within our reach and acquisition, we cannot commit a greater mistake, a greater act of folly, than to keep him at a distance, and to refuse his offices of love and kindness. Yet how often is this mistake committed! How often do we see men making the least welcome those who have the highest title to their confidence, because they would do them real good; and treating as most welcome those whose influence on them is painfully prejudicial. The man who would not allow David in his sight, promoted Doeg the Edomite, and allowed him to stand in his presence. But he who acted thus stands before us, by his own confession, as a monument of folly. Have you, among those with whom you are conversant, one who has given proof of affectionate interest in your welfare, who has laid himself out for your good, who has borne with your temper, and when unfairly treated has returned again to the attempt to serve you, and to promote your highest happiness? Have you ever, like Saul in reference to David, felt the risings of dislike to your friend, because, in some form or another, he seemed to stand in the way of your cherished plans and self-gratifying projects? Have you meditated having nothing more to do with him, putting a barrier between yourself and him by some decisive act? Have you shown, and are you intent upon showing, that your preferences lie in another direction? Beware how you listen to the suggestions of the evil spirit. You may deprive him of the opportunity of intercourse with you; you may, by some javelin aimed at his peace – his comfort – his heart, succeed in driving him to a distance, and keeping him there; you may supply his place with another more to your mind: but you may also live to look back on your act, and to mourn bitterly, as you feel that he whom you repulsed was your friend after all, and your best friend too; and to exclaim, as the tears of remorse chase each other down your care-worn cheeks, "I have played the fool, and have erred exceedingly."

2. Saul's folly consisted, not simply in treating as an enemy the man who was really his best friend, but in attempting, by this very conduct towards David, to fly in the face of those divine arrangements to which, however humiliating their character, he was bound, in meekness, to have submitted. God had assigned the kingdom to David: Saul was determined to keep it for himself and his family. God called upon him to yield to a privation which was in every point of view just: he determined to be the head of a reigning family. With what beautiful meekness Jonathan acquiesced is shown to us in that touching interview between himself and the friend whom he "loved as his own soul," when they met for the last time in the wilderness of Ziph in a wood, and when they made a covenant together, and Jonathan said: "Fear not: thou shalt be king over Israel, and I shall be next unto thee." (*1 Samuel 23:17*). But it was the one purpose of Saul's life to defeat God's arrangement; and nothing promised so readily and directly to accomplish his object as the death of David, and this became, therefore, the one great point at which he aimed. Yet never does a man commit himself to a harder, and at the same time

more fruitless, enterprise than when he fights against God's providential arrangements – when, for instance, God is evidently calling on him to give up some plan of his own, some scheme for his own exaltation or for his family's aggrandisement, and he will persist in carrying on that plan, whatever it may cost – when God is requiring him to take a humbler level, and he will grasp tightly and hold tenaciously the position which everything combines to tell him is not for himself nor his family, but for another. Nothing, too, is a greater temptation to a man to do unprincipled things, to allow his evil passions to have their sway, than the attempt to evade or to alter the course which events plainly show to be God's providential arrangement. But it is a fruitless work, however long maintained. "My counsel," saith the Lord, "shall stand, and I will do all my pleasure;" and as when – after his long-continued efforts to keep the succession in his own family by destroying David, – Saul found that all his excitement, all his irritation, all his determined pursuit, all were in vain, because God resisted him at every point – as, when reviewing the course he had taken, he was compelled to confess, "I have played the fool, and have erred exceedingly," – so will it ever be with those who will not yield to the intention of the Great Disposer, but venture to shape a course for themselves, involving opposition to His will. "Their folly shall be made manifest to all men;" and not less shall it be felt by themselves. Submission, which they would not render voluntarily to One who has a just right to claim it, will be wrung out of them reluctantly by One against whom "none ever hardened himself and prospered." Oh! how much would Saul have saved himself, if he had humbly bowed to the decision by which the kingdom was transferred from his own family to that of Jesse; and how much would men save themselves now, if they would resign their will to God's, especially where, as in the case of Saul, the arrangements in which they are required to acquiesce are undoubtedly disciplinary, and intended to bring down the pride of their spirits – "to lay them low and keep them there."

Against these forms of grievous folly and error, then, let us make it our prayer that we may be preserved. Saul's example shows that, once indulged, they may grow upon us, acquiring strength from day to day, until, as we look back on our course, they shall meet our view as the main characteristics of a life which might have been marked by happier features, and distinguished by holier principles. Trifle not with the friendship of those who consult your best welfare, though they may seem to stand in the way of your self-gratification. The friends who, against their own worldly interests, will be faithful to you, who will stand between you and impending spiritual peril, let them be welcome to your side, drive them not from you to make way for those who shall stand in the same relation to them as Doeg did to David. And oh! remember that

> *"One there is, above all others,*
> *Best deserves the name of Friend!"*

He is the true David – David's Son and David's Lord. For you He has faced a fiercer foe than Goliath. For you He has gained a glorious victory, and wrought a great salvation. With you He will come and dwell. When you have difficulties, He will counsel. When you have gloom, He will cheer. His voice shall be music more melodious than "David's harp of sweetest sound." Let Jesus be your Friend; never treat Him unkindly. Never let His place be vacant: and if you have grieved Him, follow after Him in penitence; pursue Him in prayer. Ask Him back, and tell Him that you "have erred exceedingly." Remember, too, that it is He, whom God has appointed to hold the throne – the throne of your heart. Do not stand out against the rightful claims of the true David. Venture not to keep for yourself, or for any object of earthly affection, that which is His due. Have you hitherto resisted this arrangement? As you look back on your life, do you feel that you have done the Saviour this injustice? Then confess your error while there is time to rectify it, and *stand by your confession.*

Saul, alas! admitted his error, but took no steps to turn his confession to practical advantage. Let us be careful against such a neglect. Are we conscious that we have reason to confess our want of wisdom, manifested in any such forms as have been under consideration? Let us proceed at once, by God's blessing, to act out on convictions. Yes! *at once,* lest the brief remainder of our life should pass away unimproved; and the words of Saul, though used by us now in confession, should continue as true in our last moments as, notwithstanding the time given for reformation, they were true in his case till his latest breath, "Behold, I have played the fool, and have erred exceedingly."

Chapter 10
The Witch of Endor

"Then said the woman, Whom shall I bring up unto thee? And he said, Bring me up Samuel." (*1 Samuel 28:11*)

THE lightning-flash has passed away, and now the gloom is all the deeper. We were startled by that flash which, as we watched it, revealed in a moment the painful whole of Saul's sad history, and drew from his lips the humiliating confession, "I have played the fool, and have erred exceedingly." And as we open the next page of the narrative, we become conscious of the succeeding gloom which is settling on his guilty and undone spirit. Upward and all around he looks for some star of hope, some heavenly lamp which might let down its genial light upon his path; but he looks in vain. Depressed and despairing, the very glare of a meteor would be a relief, as for a moment it should pierce the thickening darkness.

Tidings have reached him – tidings which demand, upon his part, prompt and energetic action. Ill-qualified is he to hear that the Philistines are mustering all their forces, and gathering in full strength, to avenge on Israel past defeat and disgrace. The occasion required a mind unembarrassed, and a spirit buoyant and free. He did, as heretofore, place himself at the head of his people, and led them to mount Gilboa; but when the far-spreading encampment of the enemy broke upon his view, his jaded spirit sank within him, terror laid hold upon him – "he was afraid, and his heart greatly trembled." His own infatuation in treating David as his enemy had much to do with the spectacle which he now beheld. Well was it known that he had wasted his energies in the murderous pursuit of the man who had laid Goliath low; and hope revived in the hearts of the Philistines when they saw that Saul had repulsed David from himself and his service. And could he send a glance along that host, eager for battle and bent on retaliation, and not remember the day when there was only one in all Israel who had dared to face the haughty Philistine as he defied the living God? Where was the stripling now who, declining other armour save that of divine defence, looked calmly on the overwhelming force, and met the advancing champion's threat with that reply, so full of exalted courage, and yet so marked by simple dependence upon heavenly support, "Thou comest to me with a sword, and with a spear, and with a shield: but I come to thee in the name of the Lord of hosts, the God of the armies of Israel, whom thou hast defied." (*1 Samuel 17:45*). Where was that youngest, ruddy-faced son of Jesse now? Ah! would that now he were here, though the tint upon his cheek had grown pale beneath the influence of a few more years of life's cares and duties, and some furrows on his brow already proclaimed that his heart had been no stranger to anxiety. Never was his presence more desirable: never did the unhappy king more need his generous services. For his absence Saul's guilty conscience could best assign the reason. But was there none beside to whom he could look for guidance – to whom he could submit the anxious questions which were now pressing on him – who could advise him how to arrange the host – how to plan his movements – whether he should make the attack or wait to receive it – and who could speak some words of hope, and cheer him with some calculations of the probability of success? Like many others, in the hour of sorrow he remembered God; and the memory of those early days came back when all such questions would have been referred *directly to God Himself* – when instructions from the court of heaven would have relieved his mind, and caused him to go forth comforted, because the battle was the Lord's. The messenger who used to bear those directions no longer survived. Samuel had been gathered to his fathers. Grieved at heart by the perverseness and folly which had characterised one from whom better things might have been expected, wearied by the continual rejection of his admonitions, and disappointed in the bright hopes which he had cherished, he had retired from the post of the king's adviser, and had betaken himself to his quiet and peaceful home at Ramah. Not that he then forgot Saul; ah, no! he "mourned for" him; for he had often looked on him with a loving eye, had breathed over him the utterances of a loving heart, and he could not see him go astray and forsake his own mercies and sin against his own soul, without experiencing those deep and distressed emotions which those best know who have made the highest interests of others the constant object of their solicitude, but who have been doomed to see their efforts rendered useless by a perverseness which would not listen to reason, and a haughtiness which set the voice of friendship at defiance. We cannot affix a darker stain on our character than to have contributed to embitter the days – and especially the last days – of those who loved us, than to have rendered them mourners on our account, who might have drawn their joy and comfort from the consistency of our daily walk. Had there been a far less circumstantial narrative of Saul than that which we do possess, his condemnation would have been sufficiently embodied in those telling words, "Samuel came no more to see Saul: nevertheless *Samuel mourned for Saul.*"

To these sorrows and cares death had now put an end; and the people, conscious of the greatness of their loss, and weeping over their bereavement, had laid him in the tomb in his own city of Ramah. Had the prophet been living, Saul would now have sought a message from the Lord through him. Some word from God, however, he felt that he must have – it was his only resource. He could not, dared not, proceed without it. The school of the prophets, who had been brought up at the feet of Samuel, suggested itself to his mind; through some of the disciples he might derive the heavenly direction which he could no longer gain through their master. He made application, but "the Lord answered him not by the prophets." The priests – could they help him? Still in their possession was the breastplate of judgment, glittering with its precious stones; and the chief priest put on his holy garments, his ephod and its girdle, and the sparkling jewels on his breast, and went in and stood before the Lord, an enquirer for his unhappy sovereign. But no response came forth from the holy place; "the Lord answered him not by Urim." There might be still, the monarch thought, some other form in which the will of God might be made known. He remembered how that "in a dream, in a vision of the night, when deep sleep falleth upon men, in slumberings upon the bed; then God openeth the ears of men, and sealeth their instruction," (*Job 33:15, 16*), and his discouraged heart found comfort in the thought that perhaps God would give *him* instruction thus. But "the Lord answered him not by dreams." Terrible, indeed, was the lesson which he was learning now, and it is one which has lost none of its awfulness by the passing of time. That repeated, that disappointing refusal had a voice, and it taught, it reiterated a truth of which Saul had received sufficient intimation before – that those who do not take God's counsel when He gives it, will not be able to obtain it when, with an agonising sense of their necessity, they come at length to implore it.

With the sad spectacle before us of Saul's importunity, ending only in dreariest disappointment, we hear the tones of Wisdom uttering her words, and saying, "Because I have called, and ye refused; I have stretched out my hand, and no man regarded; but ye have set at nought all my counsel, and would none of my reproof: I also will laugh at your calamity; I will mock when your fear cometh; when your fear cometh as desolation, and your destruction cometh as a whirlwind; when distress and anguish cometh upon you. Then shall they call upon me, but I will not answer; they shall seek me early, but they shall not find me: for that they hated knowledge, and did not choose the fear of the Lord: they would none of my counsel: they despised all my reproof. Therefore shall they eat of the fruit of their own way, and be filled with their own devices." (*Proverbs 1:24-31*). Can we hear these words, and not discern an instance of their truthfulness in the utterly unavailing character of all Saul's efforts to gain an answer of direction from the Lord? And can we see them illustrated in his sad history, and not dread, lest, if we pursue his course of determined rejection of God's counsel in the days of comparative prosperity, we should find ourselves involved in his disappointment and punishment in the days of adversity?

It was a desperate thought which at this juncture arose in the mind of the king – a thought which, however, showed how far he was from perceiving, or if he in any manner perceived it, how far he was from allowing himself to be influenced by, the real cause of his present perplexity. God had forsaken him; but he acted not as though he attached any blame to himself as being the cause of this silence on the part of heaven. He appears to have merely ascribed it to the fact that Samuel was not alive to be the enquirer for him at the mouth of the Lord, and to receive for him the message of the Most High.

He said not, Oh! that I had listened while Samuel was living; but he said, If only that favoured prophet were here, God would hear him, and I should gain my point. The prevailing characteristic of his life was roused into action once more. He would not be thwarted, even by the arrangements of God's providence. He would have his own way, cost what it might. He would have an answer. Samuel had passed into the world of spirits; he would fetch him back; and the information he could acquire from no other sources, he would now seek through him. It was, indeed, presumption without a parallel – an expedient to which only despair could have ever conducted him. And yet the very thought implied a striking testimony to Samuel's worth, and indicated a state of mind ready and willing to repose confidence now in one whom he had mortified by his folly, and driven from him by his disobedience.

He could not ask that God would lend His aid to carry out this interference with the unseen world: there was another method to which he must betake himself, in order to secure the end upon which, as upon a last resource, his mind was now set. It was with strange inconsistency, indeed, that he who had put away those who had familiar spirits and the wizards out of the land, addressed his servants – "Seek me a woman that hath a familiar spirit, that I may go to her, and enquire of her." The request gives us a proof sufficiently plain that the part which Saul had acted in putting down witchcraft did not proceed from disbelief in the reality of the powers professedly assumed by those against whom he had directed his decree, nor from a principled regard to those laws which, given by the hand of Moses, had declared that a man or a woman who had a familiar spirit should "surely be put to death:" "There shall not be found among you an enchanter, or a witch, or a charmer, or a consulter with familiar spirits, or a wizard, or a necromancer." (*Deuteronomy 18:10, 11*). In the suppression of this class he had, in all probability, acted simply from selfishness. His act arose either from a desire to be thought religious, or from a suspicion that the evil spirit which troubled him came by their machinations, or from fear lest these arts might, in some new form, be practised against him. The measure which he took for the extermination of witchcraft had not, however, been wholly successful; and at Endor, a town belonging to the tribe of Manasseh, and four miles south of Tabor, a woman who professed to have intercourse with the invisible world still pursued her magic arts, and the circumstance appears to have been well-known to the servants of Saul. Encamped, as his army was, in Gilboa, the residence of this woman was within his reach, and he prepared himself to go and solicit her aid in his difficulty. It was evening; and the hours of that day had passed heavily, anxiously along; not a moment of peace had he known, not a morsel of food had he tasted, when, summoning all the strength he yet possessed, he put on other raiment that he might not be recognised, and, attended by two servants, went forth on that errand which was as wicked as it was humiliating. Night found them at the impostor's door; and with hurried tone and beating heart the woman, little suspecting by whom she was addressed, was engaged to render her services in calling a departed spirit from the next world. She did what was natural in providing for secrecy; and with a view of ascertaining how far the unknown applicant was to be trusted, she acted her part well in affecting to suppose that the presence of her three visitors was part of a plan to detect her in an unlawful occupation, and to ensure her punishment. But who shall say with what a sting the conscience of that unhappy man was made to smart, as he heard her say, "Thou knowest what Saul hath done, how he hath cut off those that have familiar spirits, and the wizards, out of the land: wherefore then layest thou a snare for my life, to cause me to die?" (*1 Samuel 28:9*). Assured, however, by his solemn oath that no harm should come to her, the woman proceeded at once to the matter of business in reference to which application had been made to her. But never was that system of wicked imposture which she practised, and which her royal but wretched visitor now patronised – never was it more signally punished – never was presumptuous crime rendered more completely the means of overwhelming the perpetrator – never was the truth more clearly exemplified, "thine own wickedness shall correct thee," than at that moment when – having asked who was to be brought up – the answer of Saul, "Bring me up Samuel," had scarce escaped his lips, before there arose, to her alarm and dismay, the very form of the old prophet; and she screamed with fright as for once she saw the thing really done which she had deluded so many by professing she was able to do – and done so quickly, that it was impossible that either she or her visitor could ascribe it to any act of her own performance. Insulted by her long-continued traffic in deceit and lies, provoked by the desperate presumption of the man who asked the aid of her arts, that God who has the keys of the invisible world, who openeth and none can shut, and shutteth and none can open – that God for whom nothing is too hard – that God who never more severely visits sinners than when he permits them to reach the ends which they have unlawfully sought – had allowed the desire of the king to be realised, but to the utter confusion of the instrumentality by means of which he had expected its accomplishment. Such is the conclusion to which we are led by the literal rendering of the passage. The original of *1 Samuel 28:12*, has no word for "when," inserted in our version, and the sentence rightly translated stands, "Then said the woman, Whom shall I bring up unto thee? And he said, Bring me up Samuel. And *the woman saw Samuel,* and she cried with a loud voice: and the woman spake to Saul, saying, Why hast thou deceived me? for thou art Saul," – thus clearly conveying the impression that no sooner had Saul spoken than Samuel was present; while, at the same moment, and in the same supernatural way, she was made aware of the royal dignity of her visitor. Awestruck, and alive to the fearful responsibility he had incurred, yet not himself venturing to look in the direction of the spot at which the woman stood, the king, affrighted as he was, strove to calm the woman, "Be not afraid: for what sawest thou?" Her answer – not, indeed, as we have it in our version, but, as it might be fairly rendered – bespeaks a mind bewildered, and yet unable to conceal from itself the fact that a power beyond and far above her own was at work: "I saw God," said she, "ascending out of the earth." Still not daring to encounter a spectacle which had so daunted the necromancer, Saul asked, "What form is he of?" And the answer left him in no doubt of the person whose appearance had thus struck terror into the heart of the deceiver – "An old man cometh up; and he is covered with a mantle." Again the words of the original, in *verse 14*, confirm the opinion that this was a real appearance of the prophet, for they tell us, when he ventured to look, that "Saul perceived that it was Samuel *himself.*" Stooping down with his face to the ground, he bowed before the prophet. But, ah! no solace was provided for the miserable sovereign in that unearthly interview. In answer to Samuel's enquiry, he told his gloomy tale, only to hear from him, in return, the announcement of deeper woe – that he had made God his enemy, that the malignant purpose of his own heart against David would be defeated, that his army would be beaten, and that his days were numbered, for that, on the morrow, the veil of the invisible world which he had presumptuously sought by wicked arts to draw aside for the egress of the prophet's spirit, would be drawn aside again, for the entrance of himself and his sons: "Tomorrow shalt thou and thy sons be with me." His mission ended, these few sad words of rebuke and terror uttered, Samuel was seen no more. Such was the extraordinary interview. The record of it appears to be so constructed as to produce on our minds the deep impression of Samuel's real appearance, and to leave us under no necessity of ascribing anything that transpired, either to Satanic agency, or to the necromancer's jugglery. Regarding this visit from the unseen world as a matter of fact, and as an interposition of the Most High, we can trace important ends which would be answered by it, beyond the announcement of doom to the guilty king. Not the least valuable among these results would be – to confirm, under that ancient dispensation, the belief in a future state, by the actual appearance of one who rose from the dead – to restrain the habit of applying to the professed practisers of witchcraft with a view of gaining insight into the secrets of the next world, and to indicate the supremacy of the God of Israel, and his real possession of power over the tenants of the unseen state.

Conclusions such as these, which would naturally follow from the occurrence, and which would suggest themselves powerfully wherever intelligence of the event was diffused, are so opposed to any purpose which Satan would desire to promote, that we find in this very opposition sufficient reason, even if there were no other, for not attributing the appearance of Samuel to demoniacal agency. On the other hand, to adopt that view of the case which denies the real appearance of the prophet, while it makes the woman cajole Saul into the idea that he was there, and carry on a conversation in the person of Samuel, is to overlook, as we think, the repeated affirmation that it was Samuel – *Samuel himself* – is to disregard the plainness of the narrative, which gives us no idea but that the facts transpired as they are here told; and is, most certainly, to open the way to confusion in the interpretation of Scripture, by giving liberty to treat other incidents as not being real transactions, but only imaginary scenes. But more; it is to leave several circumstances unaccounted for, which are easily explicable if we regard the visit of Samuel as a real interposition of God; it is to leave unanswered the questions, How the woman became so awfully terrified at that which, after all, on the supposition of mere trickery, had nothing in it to frighten her? How, in this case, the effect was produced before she had time to use a single art? How she came to know, in a moment, that it was Saul, and to be so certain as to tell him that she knew him? How she could be sure that the Philistines would be victorious? How she could be certain that he would die on the morrow, and that his sons would die with him?

The sequel of the interview is most affecting. Worn by anxiety – consumed by inward care – and weakened by the previous day's abstinence from food, Saul was in no condition to sustain the shock which had come upon him in the announcement that his army would be defeated, and that he himself, with his sons, would soon be numbered with the dead – that message from the unseen world before which the stoutest heart would have quailed, and by which the strongest nerves would have been unstrung. He trembled – faltered – fell upon the ground – and lay there, fainting and helpless. In vain, at first, did the woman and his attendants implore him to take food. At length, they lifted him from the ground, and placing him on the couch, prevailed upon him to eat. But time was flying fast; it must not be known that he had been at Endor; and lest the secret should be discovered, he arose while the gloom of night, yet unbroken, afforded the opportunity of concealment, and, with his attendants, went away.

"Tomorrow thou shalt be with me." The words, as spoken by the prophet, refer simply to the invisible state, without allusion to that distinction of conditions which, under the advanced and enlarged teaching of the Christian dispensation, we know to follow *immediately* on the entrance of spirits into the next world. "Tomorrow thou shalt be with me." How must those words have haunted the guilty soul of Saul as he retraced his steps to the encampment! What fearful forebodings – what agonising anticipations! And soon it was "*tomorrow,*" – the first faint streak was seen in the east – the morning dawned – the darkness fled away. Mount Tabor, rearing its head in the distance, caught the bright beams of the rising sun, and the mountain ridges on the south of Esdraelon were gilded by its cheerful rays.

But external nature cannot always produce upon the mind that which would appear to be its natural and legitimate reflection. Its most soothing and tranquillising aspects may have no power to calm the disquieted spirit, and may but serve to show

"How ill the scene that offers rest,
And heart that cannot rest, agree."

And the mind may be in no condition to be invigorated by nature's fresh and reviving beauty, to be gladdened by the morning, as it tinges with a joyous glow surrounding scenes and objects. The very beams which shine on these to brighten and to cheer, may fall upon the heart, morbid and melancholy, only to give it and to fix upon it a darkness deep and decisive, and to leave behind the hue of sadness. Just as in experimenting on the chemical agency of light, we find that there are certain circumstances, under which the very rays of the sun itself falling on an object, will make its colour black. Say, does the early brightness make the felon's heart lighter or darker on the morning of his execution? Is he cheered, as his eye catches its brilliance? or, rather, is not his spirit all the heavier? "*Tomorrow*" sank heavily in his heart, as he heard it pronounced yesterday; and all the fairness of the sun, and all the freshness of the morning, have but one voice to him – that now that "tomorrow" has arrived, that fatal "tomorrow." It was even thus with Saul. Ah! what a night he had passed! The early breeze struck chill upon his fevered soul; and his heart, saturated with bitterness, met the morning sun only to have a deeper, darker gloom infused and deposited there. Think what it must have been to have left his tent with the thought, "I shall never return;" to have marshalled his host with the awful conviction, "I am going to die;" to have looked on his sons as he assigned them their positions, and to have been sure that to them the issue would be fatal; and when the armies met, and the shout of battle rose, to have heard amidst it all, and louder far than all, the echo from his inmost soul of that dreadful, unearthly utterance of the night before, "Tomorrow shalt thou be with me."

Solemn – deeply solemn – are the instructions to be gained from the incidents which have now passed in review before us.

1. To one of these, allusion has been already made in a preceding chapter, but it is so important that it may well claim repeated notice. We mean this – that we may have taken strong ground against some

particular form of evil, we may have condemned it in others, and we may, thus far, have acted outwardly in consistency with God's commands; but we may live to do the very thing which we have condemned, to break the very commands to which we have given an external homage. And why? Because the native rebellion of the heart against God has not been subdued; because the principle of holy obedience – that principle which directs itself against *all* sin on account of its inherent evil, its offensiveness in the sight of God – has never been sought and implanted. There may be motives for putting away one particular form of sin, the operation of which may yet co-exist with a spirit unwilling to yield to the fear of God, and unaffected by his love. It was not because Saul's heart was prepared to render allegiance to God that he put away witchcraft; it was not because he saw in it an awful sin against the Most High; but because he would affect an outward regard for religion, or because he wished to avenge his mental disquietude on those whom he deemed its cause, or because he was in daily fear of some further mischief from them. The operation of these motives, and their result, still left him a rebel, prepared at any time, when the will of God crossed his own purpose, to resist the commands of the Almighty. His own character underwent no change in carrying out this crusade against the wizards. His rebellion, in the sight of God, was as bad as their witchcraft. That crime was a form in which the spirit of rebellion was embodied. And wherever the spirit of opposition to the divine will is permitted, there is no security against its indulgence in any particular form; and if circumstances arise to make it convenient, it may develop itself in the identical manifestation which, in a previous stage of our history, we have been most ardent and loud in condemning. Let us be assured that no outward reformations are to be depended on, which do not issue from that radical change of which the Holy Spirit is the author, and in which the whole heart is yielded up to God; in which all sin is seen to be sinful; in which there are no reserves in favour of anything which God has forbidden. Rather we might say, that a reformation on some one particular point, effected without this radical change, carries in it the very elements of weakness; it deludes the soul into an idea of its own sufficiency; and while leading, as it did in the case of Saul, to self-satisfaction, it destroys the motives for circumspection, prayer, and dependence on God, and thus, too often, paves the way to greater acts of delinquency. Let us be earnest, then, in seeking a thorough change of heart, as the only effectual spring of right conduct and of permanent reformation. Let us not indulge opposition to God in one shape, while we are condemning it under another, lest the temptation to that which we condemn should arise in our own circumstances, and the proof of the existence of a really unsanctified heart should be discovered in our living to practise that which we have been accustomed loudly to censure. How frequently have the lessons now before us been confirmed by actual instances! How often have we seen the man who was sternly severe against commercial dishonesty – who prided himself upon honour and integrity in business – unable, when pushed by circumstances, to stand against the temptation of putting a few pounds into his purse, by doing a mean and ungentlemanly trick! How sad, too, it has sometimes been to see the drunkard reel along the street, and, as we passed, to recognise the countenance of one who has been loudest in his denunciations of the intoxicating cup! How bitter to track to the haunts of vice the footsteps of the man whose lips and language have often, in our hearing, marked down impurity as an accursed thing, with which he could hold no sympathy! Yet instances such as these are but repetitions of that which occurred when Saul, the avowed opponent of witchcraft, himself went to the witch of Endor; and they are the confirmations of the principle to which his case conducts – that nothing but a radical change of heart in reference to *all* sin is an effectual preservative against the commission of *any one* sin.

2. We cannot but notice, as we review this incident, how certainly a man loses his own dignity in proportion as he recedes from the principle of obedience to God, and yields to the guidance of his own heart. What term so aptly describes the condition of the king of Israel in the witch's abode at Endor, as that of *degradation* – deep, thorough degradation. How completely lost to all self-respect he must have become! How impossible it must have been for anyone else really to respect him! How hard to recognise in that figure, as it stealthily creeps into the obscure dwelling, the tall young man whose very presence won the hearts of Israel, and so inspired them that they made him king by acclamation! Yet *sin* had caused the difference – the mighty, melancholy difference; nothing but sin – nothing but casting

off the fear of God. Obedience to divine command, submission to divine control, would have saved him from it all. Be it ours to take warning. No station in life, however exalted – no position, however respectable – no claims on the regard of society, however strong – can stand against the degrading influence of *indulged sin.* Thousands who seemed strong in their standing have lived to give fearful confirmation to this truth; and as some have hidden themselves in the hovel which has succeeded to the comfortable home, or have been stretched on the hard mattress which has succeeded to the bed of down, or have scowled in the gloomy prison which has succeeded to the abode of freedom and of peace, you have heard the sigh which broke your own heart while it arose from theirs, "To think that I should ever have come to this!"

3. We are taught that mercies abused and privileges slighted may be desired when they have been withdrawn, and when, in God's providential arrangements, they are no longer within our reach. While Samuel lived, his counsel was treated with contempt; but when he could no longer be consulted, when his voice could no longer be heard, his advice no longer be given, then the very man who grieved him most was most anxious to have him back at any cost, and was willing to adopt the most desperate, and at the same time the most humiliating, measures, in order to gain just a very few moments of intercourse with him. Listening to the expression of that desire, "Bring me up Samuel," we feel the rising of a wish, "Would that the living prophet had been allowed his rightful influence; then there would have been no necessity for recalling him when dead." And was not this the agonising thought which, like a poisoned dart, transfixed the inmost soul of the king himself at the moment: "Had I but adhered to his advice – had I but listened to his entreaty – had I but been moved by his tears – had I but repented and humbled myself at his expostulations – never had I been driven to desire him now, even from the dead."

Let the sad spectacle awaken enquiry, How are you employing present mercies? Shall the time ever come when you would give all you possess for a single half-hour with that earthly counsellor, that pious parent, or that anxious pastor, whose advice now follows you from day to day, from Sabbath to Sabbath, only to be treated with neglect; but when, if such a wish were gratified, it must needs be by the re-appearance from the dead of those whose very forms would be invested with so many associations of deep concern for your welfare, and prayerful solicitude for your peace? But no! that wish will come too late, when the grass shall have grown high upon their graves, and the green moss shall have gathered on their tomb-stones; it will come too late when in that world whose duration is not measured by days and years, and where the sun never goes down, their spirits, emancipated from sin and care, shall have long become accustomed to the notes of celestial music and the forms of heavenly service. Besides, if they were to return, what reason would there be to expect that, after the excitement of such a visit were over, you would be more willing to yield to their counsel then than you are now, when with assiduous care they watch your path, and with frequent tears beseech you to be reconciled to God? The heart that can stand out against present tenderness and prayers and pleadings, gives fearful reason to expect that it could stand out against any means, the most extraordinary, which might be employed to move. And if they were to return, they could tell you nothing more which is needful to be known, in order to induce you to give yourself to God and to his service, than you now possess: "If they hear not Moses and the prophets, neither will they be persuaded, though one rose from the dead." (*Luke 16:31*).

Yet, oh! if some of those who have already fallen asleep in Jesus could but visit for an hour these lower scenes; if some of those who were known as the most active members of the Christian commu-nity with which they were associated – the prayerful fathers and the anxious mothers, the men, the women, whose holy example shed radiance all around, whose houses had an altar and a flame of devotion burning brightly there; who taught their children also, and said unto them each and often, "Get" heavenly "wisdom, get understanding: neither decline from the words of our mouth;" who pointed them to the celestial city, and themselves led the way – if some of these could visit their earthly homes again, could spend a day or night among those very children who were the subjects of so many prayers, the recipients of so many counsels, what altered scenes would meet them! How completely, in too many instances, would they be conscious of the lack of that element of spiritual religion which was the very atmosphere which they breathed! How entirely would they miss the altar which their reverence for God had reared, and their prayerful habits had maintained! How horror-struck would they be to find the giddy dance take the place of cheerful and instructive intercourse, the worldlings' assembly in those very rooms where Christians used to meet, and be welcomed with a smile that said,

> "These are the company I keep,
> These are the choicest friends I know."

And would not tones of sadness and of condemnation be elicited from them, like those which fell from the venerable prophet when, at God's behest, he re-appeared to Saul? But can it be right to do that which you know would be as opposed to their feelings, could they revisit this world, as it is to their advice while they lived in it, and to their injunctions when they left it? Will you take advantage of their removal thus to trifle with the religion they loved, and to cast dishonour on the God whom they adored? Have you already done so? Are you beginning, meditating to do so? Then go and ask, what that now sainted father would see – what that now glorified mother would feel – what that departed pastor would say – could they behold your homes and know your habits? If your Bible and your conscience tell you that *their* chosen way of life was the right one, as both assuredly must and will tell you, then pause – reflect – reform. And if the thought should rise, "But, after all, they cannot know – they do not see – they are not where we are – what does it matter?" then remember that you and they will meet again – that they will rise from the dead, and you will rise too. But how will you meet them at that dread day of resurrection and of judgment? How will you look on them, and they on you if, having set aside their admonitions, and having selected for yourselves another path than that in which they walked with God, and pleaded that in it you would walk with them, and after them, till life's latest hour – how will you look on them, if the open books should give forth a record of your life of worldliness, formality, and ungodliness; and the sentence should be passed which, through a long eternity, must condemn you to misery and disgrace, while heaven's brightest honours are conferred on those from whose counsels you departed, and to whose example you allowed no weight! Let your decisions as to your duty be formed in prospect of that hour, when the "many who sleep in the dust of the earth shall awake, some to everlasting life, and some to shame and everlasting contempt." In which of these two classes will you be found? But in order to share the honours of the saints of God then, we must, in heart and habits, be united with them now.

Chapter 11

The Suicide

"Then said Saul unto his armour-bearer, Draw thy sword, and thrust me through therewith; lest these uncircumcised come and thrust me through, and abuse me. But his armour-bearer would not; for he was sore afraid. Therefore Saul took a sword, and fell upon it." (*1 Samuel 31:4*)

IT is an expressive, but a most melancholy, form which we are sometimes constrained to adopt, of pronouncing our estimate of an individual's character, when, while others are speculating as to what will be the next passage in his history, the next step in his course, we declare that, for our own part, we shall be surprised at nothing which he may do, at nothing which may happen to him; that we are prepared to hear anything, even the worst. Such cases do occur; and if, in regard to them, we stay to ask ourselves of the reason for the impression which we entertain, we shall discover that it is the result of a continued course of conduct which has grieved us at every turn; that having been taught repeatedly how vain it is to expect anything good, we are left in bitter preparedness to hear only the reverse. It is possible to have been so frequently disappointed that we dare not form another expectation for good, lest we should ensure a further disappointment.

On these grounds we may account for the circumstance of which we cannot but be conscious in arriving at the incident on which we are now to meditate – even this: that, melancholy as it is, it does not appear to startle us; deeply distressing as we must acknowledge it to be, it certainly does not excite us in proportion to its naturally awful character. The fact is, that by our previous study of Saul's life, we have acquired a preparedness to hear of it. We have pursued so long a course of painful disappointment, that in truth we expect nothing good, nothing bright; and our emotion, when we see him perish by his own hand, is rather that of grief than of astonishment; we are more sorrowful than we are surprised at his end.

We sorrow when we think how differently he might have finished his course. We call up some records which the Scriptures have preserved – records of the manner in which the hopes of the morning of life have been realised in the calmness and setting glory of its evening hours, and we find here a painful contrast.

Could we, on the day in which Saul stood before the people, so gifted with natural endowments, and so goodly to look upon – could we then have drawn out the character of the concluding scenes of his career, framed according to our wishes and our hopes – and had the sketch thus drawn been realised in fact, how opposite a narrative to that which we are now contemplating would have found its place on the page of sacred history! For such a sketch our wishes would have borrowed – and in it our hopes would have included – the sweet tranquillity, the holy confidence, with which the favoured son of Jacob yielded up his spirit, speaking with his dying lips the words of solace to those whom he left behind him, "Behold, I die: but God will visit you." We should have united with this the tender anxiety for the nation's future peace which marked the departing hours of Joshua. We should have interwoven with these the dignified assertion of personal and judicial integrity with which Samuel reviewed his tenure of office; and combining all these, we should have felt that they would constitute the fitting features for the close of a public life which, like Saul's, had begun so auspiciously. We might, too, have reasonably hoped that, welcome as Saul was made to draw largely on divine resources – that, identified as his kingdom was with the "Great King," "the Lord of hosts," his efforts for its protection and preservation would have been so successful as that there would have been no more invasion attempted by his enemies, and that his last moments would have been cheered by the thought of his people sitting beneath their vines and their fig trees, none daring to make them afraid. And had the thought of another and a different kind of public solemnity occurred on the day to which we are referring, had we anticipated the moment when that fine form would be stretched in death, and carried to the silent tomb, our wishes would, undoubtedly, have framed a funeral scene such as was afterwards realised in the case of another king of the chosen tribes; we would have had him buried, as was the good king Josiah, in the sepulchre of his fathers, amidst the tears of all Judah and Jerusalem; some prophet should have lamented him; and some later historian should have told how, even down to his own day, "all the singing men and singing women spake of" Saul "in their lamentations," and how all "this was made an ordinance in Israel."

But if these had been our hopes and anticipations on that auspicious day on which the son of Kish was hailed as king, the prospect would have soon become dim; and as his first wrong step was succeeded by instances of more determined departure from God, these visions of hope would have been more and more beclouded, until at length there would not have been discerned a single ray of cheerfulness in all our thoughts of the future. It is sad to feel it, and to say it, but we are conscious of a certain naturalness of connection between Saul's life and his death. The end of his course has a melancholy, an awful agreement with all the preceding stages, after he had once wandered from the right path, and given himself to the act, to the habit, of setting up his own will in opposition to the commands of God. It is what we are prepared to expect.

Still it is important for those practical purposes which we have had in view in studying this portion of Scripture history, that we should notice that no degree of preparedness to receive intelligence of such an event as that in which the career of Saul terminated, at all detracts from its intrinsic awfulness. It was self-destruction of the most determined kind; he would have consented to the use of another's hand, but that hand would have been impelled by himself; and when he could not gain his end in a way which would have made another a murderer, but would not any the less have fixed on him the crime of suicide, he took his own sword, and falling on it, sunk in death on the battlefield.

There is always something solemn in doing things which, when done, cannot be undone – in taking steps which, when taken once, can never be recalled. We are conscious of this, even in those cases in which the associated circumstances are those of personal

pleasurableness or advantage; even there a feeling of deep serious-
ness comes over us as we do the decisive act, and think it cannot be
revoked. We sign our contracts with a trembling hand; and enter into
those bonds which least of all we desire to break, with a solemnity
which arises from the thought that, once entered upon, we cannot
recede. But if, in regard to procedures which have only that about
them which tends to satisfaction, we find that the impossibility of
retreating produces this order of feelings, how much more must they
be associated, in our view, with the deliberate and wilful taking of a
step which has no sooner become an actual fact, than it conducts to
consequences the most fearful, to ruin the most tremendous! How
horrified should we be if, as we were climbing some Alpine height,
we saw a traveller in advance of us slip in a moment from the edge
of a frightful precipice, and disappear before we could rush forward
to prevent him! How would the shriek of our agony, "He has gone!
he has gone!" pierce the air, and echo from the mountain-crags –
agony which would admit of no relief, because we could never bring
him back; because before that echo had died away his life would be
extinct, and his body would be dashed in pieces. But how unspeak-
ably would our anguish be enhanced if, instead of that fall being the
result of accident, it had been a deliberate and determined act; if,
as our eye turned suddenly in the direction of the stranger, we had
noticed how, with a wretched and careworn countenance, he stood
for an instant to give a farewell look at the objects he was leaving, and
then, with a spring which showed how fully he meant what he was
doing, made the fatal leap. How bitterly, as we felt the impossibility
of bringing him back from the abyss, should we wail over the fact
that he did it himself, and that now there was no help for him.

It is with emotions of this kind that we watch the last moments
of the king of Israel. We see him falling. There is a plunge – a fearful
plunge; we miss him: he is irrecoverably gone – and he did it himself!

Yet when we contemplate such a termination of earthly existence
in the case of individuals whose latest hours of life give painful proof
of rebellion against God still unsubdued, how little, after all, do we
see as compared with the actual realities of the case. It is only the
life of the body which has been interrupted – the soul survives! The
difference between the present and the past is this – that the place of
misery is changed, but the endurance itself is continued – nay, more,

indefinitely enlarged. The wretched man on earth is converted into the lost spirit in hell, a lost spirit with a heavier burden to bear than all besides – the burden of that bitter thought, "I plunged myself into this woe; I came uncalled; I rushed unsent." The act of suicide affords the most decisive evidence of the extensive delusion which men can practise on themselves, and of the blinding power which they permit the tempter to exercise over them, when, under the idea of relief and escape, they involve themselves in a deeper calamity, and in order to effect an oblivion of present suffering, they grasp the cup of eternal woe, and put it to their lips. "From what shall I escape?" is but one-half of the question – "Into what shall I bring myself?" is the still more momentous portion of the enquiry. That step must needs be ruinous which is taken solely under the influence of the former consideration, and entirely to the exclusion of the latter. Who that listens to the sentence descriptive of Saul's fear lest he should be abused by the Philistines, but must feel the wish, "Ah! that he had been as anxious about the hereafter as he was about the present; that he had been as solicitous about the destiny of his soul as he was about the treatment of his body; that he had been as careful to avoid everlasting shame, as he was to escape the momentary mockings and taunts of the Philistines." And wherever we find our fellow-men adopting the same plan of evading and ending the sorrows of time, the same reflections will inevitably arise over the fearful and criminal mistake.

Looking at the circumstances of Saul's death in their connection with the history of the people over whom he reigned, it is impossible not to perceive that they were fraught with instruction to the nation, with lessons valuable though humiliating. They reiterate with deeper emphasis the truth which has already, in some measure, come under our consideration – that when men are determined to have their own way – when they will not listen to heavenly suggestions, to divine remonstrances – when the methods by which God would promote their happiness and peace are treated by them as insufficient – and when they think that they can manage better for themselves than God can manage for them, there is but one way of convincing them of their error. They must be allowed to take the problem of their peace and happiness into their own hands, to attempt to work it out in their own fashion, and then to reap the bitter results of failure, which in such a case are inevitable. The Israelites, alive to their national difficulties, and especially to their perpetual exposedness to foreign invasion, had formed their own theory of a remedy; and, as is most often the case under such circumstances, they became blindly attached to their theory. Their proposed remedy was, as we have seen at the commencement of the history, the possession of a king, who should lead them forth to battle, as other sovereigns placed themselves at the head of their armies. In positive terms God himself told them that their theory was unsound; but no messages which He sent, no arguments which His prophet enforced, were allowed to have any weight. They were dazzled and fascinated with the thought of the success which, under a king, would attend their arms; the victories which they would achieve for themselves; and the humiliations which they would impose on their enemies. No Philistine henceforth would boast himself against Israel; no threatening message of defiance would cause their hearts to quail. The king was given; the experiment was left in their own hands. At first – yet ah! for how short a time – it seemed to answer; the nation revived, there was apparent prosperity, and the daughters of Israel were "clothed in scarlet, and other delights;" and they ascribed it all to the influence of the new king that they had "ornaments of gold on their apparel." But time rolled on, and it became evident that something more was needed to prevent foreign invasion than the possession of a king; that there were other evils, too, which their favourite scheme could not rectify. The nearer the experiment drew to its termination, the less hopeful grew their prospects from the administration of Saul; and when, at length, he died, it was not on the field of Israel's glory and victory, but on the field of their defeat and their shame. Instead of that page in their annals which they had fondly imagined, would be written in glowing lines of national greatness attained, of territory secured, and of foes intimidated, the pen of historic fidelity was constrained to substitute another, even a record which exposed the folly of their theory, and the utter failure of their remedy for national evils. They worked out their own problem, and they brought it to this issue – "And the men of Israel fled from before the Philistines, and fell down slain in mount Gilboa ... And when the men of Israel that were on the other side of the valley, and they that were on the other side Jordan, saw that the men of Israel fled, and that Saul and his sons were dead, they forsook the cities, and fled; and the Philistines came and dwelt in them." (*1 Samuel 31:1, 7*). What now had Israel gained by preferring their own plan of an earthly sovereign to the guidance and the government, the protection and the power, of God as their king? Where now were their bright hopes and fond imaginings of what man could do for them? And thus will it ever be, where men expect to reap more from their own theories than from God's fixed laws and plans. Their persistence in their rebellion against His supremacy may provoke Him to leave them to pursue their own course, and allow them to become the immediate agents in their own failure, and then events will illustrate the truth of all that His Word has said, "He that trusteth in his own heart is a fool," (*Proverbs 28:26*). "It is better to trust in the Lord than to put confidence in man. It is better to trust in the Lord than to put confidence in princes," (*Psalm 118:8, 9*). "Put not your trust in princes, nor in the son of man, in whom there is no help. His breath goeth forth, he returneth to his earth; in that very day his thoughts perish," (*Psalm 146:3, 4*). So striking is the repetition of that lesson, of which we are reminded by the circumstances of Israel at the death of Saul – a lesson which, conveyed in precepts, is confirmed by promises on the one hand, and by threatenings on the other. "Happy is he that hath the God of Jacob for his help, whose hope is in the Lord his God," (*Psalm 146:5*). "Blessed is the man that trusteth in the Lord, and whose hope the Lord is;" but "thus saith the Lord; Cursed be the man that trusteth in man, and maketh flesh his arm, and whose heart departeth from the Lord," (*Jeremiah 17:5, 7*). Beneath this curse Israel had now fallen, and that sentence which was uttered by prophetic lips many years afterwards in the name of Jehovah, and a part of which we have already dwelt upon, affords in its concluding portion the divine comment on the last scene in the history of that sovereign whom they would have in preference to God's immediate rule and government – "I gave thee a king in mine anger, and *took him away in my wrath.*" (*Hosea 13:11*).

We may take, as a second suggestion from the spectacle before us, the thought – How dreadful it is for a man to be in trouble without God to sustain and support him. The waves and billows were indeed going over Saul. The bitter recollections called up by the transactions of the preceding evening; the evident weakness of his own army before the hosts of the Philistines, bent as these were on retaliation, and urged on by the remembrance that they had a heavy account to settle with the Israelites; the sight of his followers routed and falling down slain on mount Gilboa; the loss of his three sons; the direct attack of the enemy upon himself, arrow after arrow from their quivers hitting him and wounding him sorely – what an overwhelming combination of mental distress with bodily anguish! There was one arm, and only one, which could have sustained him beneath this heavy load. There was one Being whose voice could have calmed the tumult of his soul, and while his body was sinking beneath those fatal wounds, could yet have afforded solace to his departing spirit, and caused a beam of celestial hope to fall upon the otherwise dark valley of the shadow of death. That Being is wont to draw near in the day of calamity, and to make known to those who are in the very depths of distress the extent of His power and the plenteousness of His redemption. But here we meet with no tokens of the presence of this only Refuge, this powerful Helper, this God of compassion and graciousness. The enquiry, "Where is thy God?" – that question of which the Psalmist speaks as being tauntingly addressed to him by his worldly contemporaries – might, with more truth, and in tones of compassion, not of taunting, have been addressed to the wretched sufferer before us, "Saul, where is thy God?" – the God from whom in early life thou didst receive so many advantages – the God who gave thee so many opportunities of knowing him, loving him, serving him – the God from whom thou wast taught to hope everything, to expect everything – the God who alone can help thee – where is He now – where is thy God?" Yet this distance, this standing aloof on the part of God, this leaving Saul to himself, all this was but the result of the wretched man's own treatment of the Most High. Not until he had rejected God had he been forsaken by Him. We see here the acting out of one of those principles which regulate the divine dealings with men. If they seek Him, He will be found of them; if they forsake Him, He will cast them off for ever. "Your iniquities have separated between you and your God, and your sins have hid his face from you," (*Isaiah 59:2*). There, on the field of blood, he stood desolate, without a single divine promise dropping its balm on his wounded heart, or a single thought of peace suggested by the Spirit, the Comforter, ministering repose amid the troubles of that dark hour. And nothing else could take the place of God, could fill the void, the awful blank produced by the absence of Him who "is our refuge and our strength: a very present help in time of trouble." He *only* is the true "rock" and "salvation" of the distressed soul; and this only refuge now affording him no solace, "without God" he was "without hope." His burden was insupportable; he could endure it no longer; and as he fell on his own sword, and thus rushed out of the world, he gave the proof – a proof which has since been often repeated – that this world, without God felt as a Friend, loved as a Father, trusted in as a Refuge, is an unbearable place – that wicked men cannot endure it themselves.

Fearful as is the lesson taught us by the self-murder of Saul, it is consolatory and relieving to know that *no one need be in trouble without God* – that if ever this mournful condition be realised by us, it will not be until we have brought it upon ourselves. It will come in our case, as it did in the case of the unhappy king of Israel, as the sequel of gracious dispensations slighted, and of divine forbearance trifled with. It will come as the manifestation of wrath which we shall have treasured up by our own act and effort. But it need not come. Precious promises point out the way in which we may be delivered from any such fear: "If thou shalt seek the Lord thy God, thou shalt find him, if thou seek him with all thy heart and with all thy soul," (*Deuteronomy 4:29*). To Him "that dwelleth in the secret place of the Most High," and who "hath set his love upon Him," the promise is given; "I will be with him in trouble; I will deliver him, and honour him," (*Psalm 91:15*). In a thousand forms is it repeated in the Scriptures, that we need never be in trouble without God. "The Lord also will be a refuge for the oppressed, a refuge in times of trouble. And they that know thy name will put their trust in thee: for thou, Lord, hast not forsaken them that seek thee," (*Psalm 9:9, 10*).

Here, then, let us fix our hope – to Him let us yield ourselves; and thus, as without His friendship and His love we are not prepared for a single trial, so shall we experience that, possessed of these, we stand ready for *any* – for *every* sorrow. Let our principle be, the necessity of an interest in God's blessing for our peace. Let us adopt it *now*. Its importance may flash upon us when it is too late to profit by it. An infidel once sat down with cool effrontery, after he had swallowed poison, and putting his pen to paper, described in few words what he had done, and justified his act in terms as offensive to reason as they were insulting to the ministers of God's truth. But as he sat with his paper before him – the poison taking effect – the manuscript became blurred and blotted; yet, amid the ink-stains and the strokes of the pen which his hand could no longer guide, there were deciphered these words: "My hand trembles – my eyes grow dim – I can see to write no more – but he that would be happy should be religious."

Thirdly: we see, in Saul's case, that there is no surer sign that a man is on the high road to ruin than that his heart is hardened against divine warnings. Quickly, one after another, came solemn calls to the king of Israel to humble himself at last before God. He had distinct notice that his days were numbered – notice brief, yet long enough to have enabled him to cast himself in contrition upon God, and, confessing that he had gone away like a lost sheep, to have sought restoration and forgiveness. He had the solemn assurance that nothing now was to be hoped for from earthly schemes and projects; but there was yet an interval in which he might have prayed, "Hide thy face from my sins, and blot out all my transgressions." Scenes that were calculated to move his proud spirit, and melt him into tenderness, transpired before his eyes. He saw the fine form of his Jonathan sink in the arms of death; and scarce had he seen it before another of his children fell, and then another. We wait; and the thought rushes into our heart, "He will break down at last; he will stand out no longer. This will revive the thoughts of God. This will induce the emotions of contrition and the cry for mercy, not yet too late. This will – this must awaken." But it did not. And then it was seen that the heart which can stand out against solemn calls, against direct warning, against dispensations which throw gloom on all that is earthly, against repeated bereavements, which will stand amid them all unchanged, perhaps even vaunting its own high-spiritedness, stands really on the very verge of ruin, and only wants a whisper from the tempter – a momentary suggestion from its own inward corruption – and the Spirit of God being grieved, and His restraining grace being removed, ruin will be the result. "He, that being often reproved hardeneth his neck, shall suddenly be destroyed, and that without remedy," (*Proverbs 29:1*).

It is a grievous miscalculation, moreover, which men make, when, conscious that life is passing on in the neglect of God and of duty, they reckon within themselves upon a certain power which they imagine the approach of death will have to awaken their attention to religious duties, and to bring with it the disposition to return to God in repentance and prayer. The entreaties of affectionate solicitude for their spiritual welfare are met by this expectation: "It will be time enough when death looks me in the face; and I have no doubt that when my last hours come, I shall be very willing to give a proper attention to those things which you represent as important. At present, I do not find the opportunity; but depend upon it that when my time arrives, you will not find me regardless and unconcerned." With such a reply as this is the minister of reconciliation put off, when he delivers the message of mercy, "Now is the accepted time." With such an answer is the fervent pleading of the Christian friend set aside. Alas! that in such a manner conscience should be satisfied and lulled to sleep. But facts are continually showing that whatever may be the tendency of approaching dissolution, of eternity drawing near, to produce impression, there is in such immediate prospects no *necessary* power to move the heart to consideration. Men lie day after day, hour after hour, knowing that they must die, watching the world receding and disappearing, and yet, even then, they often too clearly manifest that they have no desires after God, no inclination to repentance, no disposition to yield to the claims of His authority and the calls of His mercy. Was Saul moved when he knew he must die? Did his approaching end awaken his conscience, or soften his heart? Did he offer a single prayer, or breathe a single penitent wish? Nay, did not the hardening process upon his heart advance the more rapidly – more powerfully – in proportion as those very circumstances thickened around him which, it might have been thought, would have produced the very opposite effect? and did he not, in his last act, show himself to be under the influence of the same spirit of reckless disregard to the Most High, which had characterised his previous life? He "stretched forth his hand against God, and strengthened himself against the Almighty." He "ran upon him: even upon the thick bosses of his bucklers;" and his life of rebellion terminated in a deed whose very nature involves a most daring outrage upon God's prerogative and law.

God forbid that we should be resting upon the hope that, although we may now be living in disregard of the Most High and of His claims, yet that the approach of death will bring with it, as a necessarily attendant circumstance, an alteration in our thoughts and desires in a religious point of view. The indulgence of such a hope implies forgetfulness of the fact that there is only one source from which the Scripture encourages us to seek that true repentance, that change of heart and feeling, which will incline the transgressor to ask for pardon at the hand of God according to His own revealed methods of grace. That source is the immediate agency of the Holy Ghost. It is by His power that the heart of stone is removed, and the heart of flesh produced, (*Ezekiel 36:26, 27*). That Divine Spirit, who spoke through Samuel to Saul, now addresses men through the instrumentality of God's Word, enforced, as its truths are, by the dispensations of His providence. It is His whisper which conscience detects – His striving with the spirit of man which interferes for a while between men and the complete indulgence of their rebellion and unbelief. But that blessed Agent, whose mission is so lovely, whose approach is so tender, may be "grieved" by resistance, may be "vexed" by indifference, may be dishonoured by neglect, may be caused to depart by continued refusal to yield to the still, small voice, which aims at conviction, and urges to duty. How fearful a calamity this departure involves may be gathered from the prayer of the Psalmist, "Take not away thy Holy Spirit from me;" for then there will be no more impression – then there will be no more conviction; the gracious offer of "the heart of flesh" having been refused, "the stony heart" will remain, increasing in its hardness with every day's continuance; and nothing then will stir – nothing then will excite – no, not even the approach of death itself.

Here we see the mischievous mistake into which men fall. They talk as though they could ensure, in their last moments, a result which, under any circumstances, only the Spirit of God can bring about. They act as though that Divine Agent were at their control; as though that great and glorious Spirit were bound to consult their convenience. They overlook the fact, that every whisper of conscience unheeded involved a slight upon Him; every impression of Divine truth neglected was a rejection of Him; that every right emotion called up by Divine providence, but allowed to die away, was indifference practised towards Him. They cause Him to depart; and then, as though they had been guilty of no crime, they presume that, at the last, they can recover what He alone can produce, and command what none but Himself can bestow. But for these things God does visit; and when you see that the thought of death does not soften, that the stubborn insensibility of life is continued even in immediate prospect of dissolution, that spiritually all remains dull and cold, that there is no self-abasement before men, and no contrition before God, you see that it is possible to "quench" the Spirit of God, and by the rejection of His calls in the days of health and strength, actually to prevent that occurrence of appropriate emotion, on which you may be reckoning, when the hour of death shall arrive.

Fourthly: as we compare the conclusion of this history with its commencement, we cannot but discover an impressive lesson as to the influence of external circumstances upon personal character. As Saul rose in his social position, he sank in his moral condition. The outward change was one which, in ordinary estimation, would be regarded as a change for the better; but it was attended by a process within him which, undoubtedly, involved a change for the worse. A year or two passed as a king, effected an alteration in his character and demeanour which was as marvellous as it was mournful. The new circumstances into which he was thrown were just those which were favourable to the development of forms of corruption natural to the human heart, but which the peculiarities of his previous condition had not been calculated to call out into action; and in the same manner as these were elicited and brought into play, the force of natural excellence was weakened and destroyed. Reverting to the time when he first comes before us – as a son serving his father, obeying his will, and consulting his interests – we can readily conceive of him continuing to move quietly and unobtrusively along the retired paths of life, his conduct marked by exemplary modesty, and his course, until his latest day, confirming all the hopes concerning him which are expressed in the words "a choice young man, and a goodly." We should scarcely have suspected the existence or the strength of those evil passions which found a home in his heart. Exposed to no temptation to pride, with no cause exciting to jealousy, and exactly in those circumstances which are the least likely to stir the feelings of ambition and determination for the mastery, we only see him amiable, affectionate, and humble. But the throne and the crown, and the newly-acquired authority, appealed to these principles of pride and ambition, gave scope to their activity, and, as will always be the case, they gathered strength by exercise, and eventually completed Saul's ruin. The suddenness of his elevation, and the greatness of his popularity, tended, too, to enhance the mischievous power with which temptation wrought – the former precluding that discipline of the mind which has often been found so helpful for safely effecting the transition from an inferior station to one which is superior; the latter inducing that self-complacency which imposes an effectual silence on the whispers of self-suspicion, and exposing him, too, to other perils, which constantly attend popularity.

It is dangerous to keep an idol for ourselves; it is not less perilous to become the idol of others. A consciousness of being the object on which the affections – the applauses – the exultations of his fellow-creatures rest, will do more than anything else to lead a man wrong. It will first induce a diminished sense of personal dependence on God. This will gradually conduct to a feeling, however disguised, of entire independence of Him; and the sure accompaniment will be, that he will neglect to pray for the grace necessary to his position. Provoking God, thus, to leave him alone, he will fall. And if popularity hinders a man from praying for himself, it robs him, too, of the prayers of those around him. For the exalted notions which they possess of their favourite must operate to place him in the room of God, and thus, not only will the gift estrange their hearts from the Giver, the creature from the Creator, but the higher the estimation they form of their idol, the less, of course, will they think of him as one who needs their prayers. It is not from the lips which are heard to say, whether in the state or in the church – "This is the man for us; this is just what we wanted; now we have what exactly suits us," – it is not from these lips that there are to be anticipated continued, fervent, and helpful prayers. It is the utterance of such sounds as these which has fallen like poisoned breath on the heart of many a one who promised well; and the corruptions of nature have been inflamed, personal prayerlessness has succeeded to personal pride, excellences of character have faded away; and, to the confusion and humiliation of those who set up the idol, it has fallen – fallen irrecoverably – before their eyes.

Thus fell Saul! the victim of inward depravity, which was unsuspected at first, where there was so much natural excellence to admire; but depravity which was brought out into activity by his altered circumstances. Was *he* to be blamed, then? it may be asked. He did not make his own circumstances. He did not seek this exaltation. It came upon him unasked, unlooked for. Must *he* be held guilty for the result? Is it consistent with the justice which the Divine Being claims as His peculiar attribute, that He should place a man in a position which shall appeal to the corrupt principles of his nature, and then that He should visit him with displeasure, because those principles having been called into activity by the temptation, have been allowed the mastery? But it is surely one thing for a man to be tempted, and another for him to yield to the temptation. There is assuredly a wide interval between the existence of natural corruption in the heart, and the forth-putting of it in the life, at the call of temptation. The latter by no means follows from the former. The grace of God stands ready to prevent the sequence. In the case of the man who has been made a partaker of that grace, it will, in answer to prayer, take up its position in front of the evil passions naturally within the bosom, so as to hinder their actual manifestation. It will operate to prevent sin having dominion. The circumstances of temptation in which such an individual may be placed will become the occasion of enlarged discoveries of the existence of natural corruption, while the dread of the possibility of this corruption becoming active by being indulged, will only be the means of inducing the soul, under the consciousness of its peril, to throw itself more humbly and entirely on the promised strength and power of God, with a view to the resistance of the temptation, and to the manifestation of the opposite principle. Hence, while in some instances we see a change in men's outward circumstances followed by a personal deterioration, do we not, in others, see it attended not less obviously by improvement in character? the reason being, that in the latter case a new position has led to self-acquaintance – it has brought to the surface unsuspected evils – it has furnished deep-felt occasion for dependence on divine grace – it has thus tended to the subjugation of internal corruption, and has strengthened to the putting forth of opposite excellence.

Whether or not a change of external position will prove a moral injury to us depends upon the state of mind in which we enter upon it; and the best preservative against its becoming thus mischievous will be found in cherishing a full conviction of the natural corruption of our hearts, accompanied by a deep sense of our entire dependence on Almighty power and grace. While, in the very nature of things, external circumstances prove temptations, by appealing to the natural evil within us, it is our comfort to know that He who, as the God of providence, has our times in His hands, meets us with the assurance that His grace is sufficient for us; "God is faithful, who will not suffer us to be tempted above that we are able; but will with every temptation also make a way of escape." (*1 Corinthians 10:13*).

And this was the lesson emphatically taught Saul from the very beginning. Never was there a man more frequently instructed in the lesson of entire dependence upon God. Supernaturally gifted at the time of his call to the throne with endowments calculated to raise the tone of his mind and feelings to the level of his kingly position, so that it could be said that he had "another heart," how forcibly was he, in that very circumstance, told that divine guidance was that which he needed, and heavenly assistance that on which he might, nay, *must*, rely. How tenderly did the venerable prophet, from the first, lead his mind to God as the source of direction – the object of confidence – the God who was to be waited for and waited upon! How complete a provision was thus made against the perils of his new position, and in favour of a course of moral elevation consistent with his outward rise in rank and station! Then must he not be held to blame for that deterioration in his character which was consequent on the change in his circumstances? From the first hour of that change he was told that he would need grace; he was told, too, where he would find it; and there was not a temptation from within, nor a mischievous influence from without, over which divine grace would not have rendered him triumphant.

A suicide, as to the life of the body, he falls on the field of blood; a suicide, as to his soul's best welfare, he rushes into the unseen world; and the moral of his end is this – that the possession of many forms of natural excellence, and the acquisition of important and interesting qualifications, may yet leave the corruptions of the heart unsubdued – that only divine grace can secure the permanence of that which is naturally excellent and estimable, and prevent its being blighted and destroyed by the power and working of inward depravity.

Then, O thou God of mercy! Source of light and truth! teach us our need of Thee. Teach us that without Thee – and away from Thee – there is no life, no peace, no safety. Make us to feel, deeply and always, that if Thou dost not keep us, we fall; that if Thou dost not save us, our own hearts will surely prove our ruin.

> *Mighty Redeemer! set us free*
>   *From our old state of sin;*
> *Oh! make our souls alive to Thee,*
>   *Create new powers within.*

Chapter 12
Tidings from Gilboa

"And David said unto him, From whence comest thou? And he said unto him, Out of the camp of Israel am I escaped. And David said unto him, How went the matter? I pray thee, tell me. And he answered, That the people are fled from the battle, and many of the people also are fallen and dead; and Saul and Jonathan his son are dead also ... And I took the crown that was upon his head, and the bracelet that was on his arm, and have brought them hither unto my lord."
(*2 Samuel 1:3, 4, 10*)

IN perusing the first chapter of the second book of Samuel – a chapter of peculiar interest, because it has handed down to us that funeral-song with which the account of Saul's personal history concludes – we meet with two circumstances which present, at first sight, the aspect of historic discrepancy. The first of these is, that the version of the Amalekite, who bore the tidings of Saul's death to David, differs most materially from that which is furnished by the historian in the last chapter of the first book of Samuel. There is little difficulty, indeed, in dealing with this matter, regarded in itself; but we draw attention to it, because there are some thoughts suggested by the points in which the Amalekite's narrative differs from the historian's, which may repay us for the careful consideration of the case. If we bear in mind the object which this stranger had in view when he addressed David, we shall very easily come to a correct conclusion as to the amount of truthfulness which is to be ascribed to his representations.

Following the course of the history, as given by the sacred writer, we had reached, in the preceding chapter, that point at which the death of the unhappy king occasioned a speedy termination to the conflict in which the Israelites were engaged against the Philistines. Many of his followers in the foremost ranks must have seen him die. They had watched how sorely he had been wounded; the pain of his body and the distress of his mind were only too evident: but even to them it must have occasioned a shock when, despair seizing fast hold of him, he fell upon his own sword, and perished by his own hand. Quickly the tidings passed from rank to rank of those who were actually fighting; till, through every part of the battlefield, it was known that their leader was no more. And then all hands began to hang down; all hearts in a moment felt that the hope of victory was gone. Confusion reigned; and flight, in the hope of personal safety, became their only thought. The neighbouring cities first, and then those further off, yielded to the panic, and a more vivid picture of thorough rout and discomfiture could hardly be drawn than is given in those words of the sacred historian, which came before us in the preceding chapter – "And when the men of Israel that were on the other side of the valley, and they that were on the other side Jordan, saw that the men of Israel fled, and that Saul and his sons were dead, they forsook the cities, and fled; and the Philistines came and dwelt in them." (*1 Samuel 31:7*).

But the horrors of the battlefield are far from terminated when the actual encounter is over, and victory has declared in favour of one of the contending parties. The after-scenes are often such as cause humanity to shudder; and to one of the most revolting of these we are introduced by the circumstances under which the tidings of Saul's death first reached David. We refer to the traversing of the field of blood, for the purpose of spoiling and plundering those who can no longer resist the hand of violence. It would appear, that soon after the fatal conflict, the body of the king of Israel was discovered by one who came early to prowl over the fearful scene, unmoved by the sight of death, undeterred by the groans of the dying. His presence thus early at the place of slaughter, though mentioned by himself as a matter of accident, was, in all probability, to be ascribed to his eager desire of anticipating the arrival of the Philistines on the morrow to strip the slain. It might be, that having, in the neighbourhood, heard of the death of Saul, or, perhaps, having even witnessed it from a distance, this Amalekite determined to turn the circumstance to his own personal advantage, and thus to gratify his covetousness. The crown and the bracelet – those insignia of royalty – might, he thought, be easily secured; and, once in his possession, they would repay his search for the body. He acted upon the thought; and, as soon as the victorious Philistines were sufficiently removed from the immediate sphere of action to leave him free to carry out his purpose undisturbed, he repaired to the spot. We seem to see him making his way among the heaps of the slain; with eager eye he peers from corpse to corpse, and pushes on, undiverted by any smaller prize, till he finds himself standing over the object for which he has been seeking. There was no difficulty in distinguishing it. That form, indeed, was as fearfully covered with wounds and with blood as any which had fallen in the slaughter, and it lay as low in the common dust. There was the imprint of the same distress on that pale countenance as had left its deep traces on many around; but the diadem and the bracelet prevented the slightest doubt that there, before him, lay the dishonoured and the defeated Saul. Speedily did the Amalekite remove the symbols of royalty; and having thus far accomplished his object, he left the bare head exposed to the winds of heaven, and flung back on the ground the arm which had been robbed without resistance of its jewel. And now, probably, it happened in this case – as it has many a time occurred in the annals of robbery and plunder – that the thing stolen has no sooner been actually obtained, than the spoiler finds its possession very inconvenient, on account of its unusual character, or extraordinary value. Had it been of less splendid material, or of less intrinsic worth, its possession would have excited no remark, and it could have been parted with without difficulty. There might be danger, too, lest it being known where a treasure so large was held by the individual who had unfairly appropriated it, the cupidity of others should be tempted at his expense. "What shall I do with this crown? and what with this bracelet?" might well be the next question as he wended his way back from the field of death; and the enquiry puzzled him. If he had gone to steal the garment of some fallen Israelite, to rob some dead body of gold which might have passed as "current money with the merchant," or if his object had been to look out for a better weapon than his own for warfare, or to gain for himself some addition to his armour, he would have felt no such difficulty as that which now beset him. But a *crown* and a *royal bracelet*, which everyone would know he could scarcely have acquired by fair means, which every Israelite would recognise as having belonged to his fallen king, and in which the Philistines, too, would have discovered a property to which they, as victors, were entitled, and of which they had been unlawfully deprived by the haste with which he had commenced his predatory excursion on the battlefield – what was to be done with these spoils? It did not answer his purpose to keep them, and yet they were far from being marketable commodities, for the ordinary ways of turning property to account were not available here.

It was at this juncture, we may suppose, that the thought occurred to him which was carried out in his interview with David. He arranged a representation of Saul's dying scene for his own convenience, taking care so to adjust its several parts as that they should exactly suit what he conceived to be David's position and feelings; and at the same time so as that they should account naturally and easily for his own possession of the royal insignia. We find him then coming to David, and while professing to sympathise with the disgrace of Israel, telling that not only were Saul and his sons dead, but that he himself had put the finishing stroke to his existence; in token of which he stood there as the bearer of the crown and bracelet. The interested part which he had to act accounts for the discrepancy between the recital which he gave, and the narrative previously furnished by the sacred writer. It was not to be expected that he should tell the truth; it was natural that such a man should pervert the facts of the case, so as to answer his own mean purpose.

In his own estimation, however, he was taking the surest way to honour and to the advancement of his worldly interests. What reward could be too large for the messenger who brought to David the intelligence of the death of his enemy? – nay, more, who had, by his own hand, put an end to the life of that bitter persecutor? Saul's death would, moreover, open up the way for David to the throne itself. It needed not much foresight to perceive that now the kingdom must be David's. What an opportunity was thus afforded for ingratiating himself with the new prince, by carrying to him the regalia of his predecessor! He could thus get rid of the spoil which he felt to be inconvenient, and could turn it to a most profitable account.

Well contrived as was the plan, it nevertheless failed; and the reason of the failure deserves notice. Many an apparently well-arranged scheme of iniquity has broken through from exactly the same cause. The Amalekite had made a grievous miscalculation as to the character of the man with whom he had to deal. He had done David a gross injustice; and he, doubtless, was not long in discovering his mistake; but then it was quite too late to recede. As he stood to tell his tale of falsehood, he saw that the countenance of the man whom he addressed did not brighten; that his heart, instead of coming out to meet him as the bearer of good tidings, was retreating further and further from him at every word he spoke, as from one for whom he felt a deep aversion. He watched the tear which started to the Hebrew warrior's eye, and he stood amazed when, trembling with very sorrow, he laid hold on his garments, and rent them. It was manifest that the news which, he had supposed, would prove the source of very substantial gratification to David, had fallen on his heart like a terrible blow, and that those around him sympathised with their leader.

His mistake was fatal. He was treated as a murderer, on his own confession; and the last words which fell on his ears were the utterances of David's indignation at the deliberate manner in which, according to his own account, he had sealed the doom of Saul: "Thy mouth hath testified against thee, saying, I have slain the Lord's anointed." He had failed in his scheme for securing his own advantage and aggrandisement, because he had formed altogether a wrong estimate of the character of David.

The incident before us gives us an opportunity of marking the immense difference in the order of mind and character which may subsist between two individuals brought together by one event, and having their attention occupied by one and the same object. And we observe, too, in this instance, a circumstance which is the natural attendant upon this diversity – the incapability, on the part of the possessor of the meaner and inferior order of mental and moral qualities, to enter into the feelings and principles of the possessor of superior endowments. This incapability operates to prevent its unfortunate subject from suspecting the existence, in a fellow-creature, of any other mode of thinking and acting than that which he himself adopts and employs; and it issues, therefore, in the habit of judging all around him by his own standard, and of reckoning that they will be actuated, in their conduct, by the principles which direct his own proceedings. The possibility that David's feelings should be what the issue proved that they were, never entered the Amalekite's mind. His own mind was evidently so debased in its views, so grovelling in its workings, that he was incapable of comprehending anything which was magnanimous and unselfish; and accordingly, he was not prepared to suppose, even, that there could exist, in David's bosom, an order of feelings superior to his own. He treated him, in his reckonings, as if he were altogether such an one as himself; he reduced him exactly to his own level. His expectation of seeing the son of Jesse shedding a tear over Saul, standing aghast at the sight of his crown, and horrified at the mode of his death, was quite as small and as distant as was any inclination, under the circumstances, to do these things himself. He judged of what David was by what his own character was, and calculated what David would do by what his own feelings would have led him to do in the case. Had he been in David's position, and had anyone brought him the intelligence of Saul's death, he would have felt that it was decidedly the best intelligence which he could have heard. Had his diadem and his bracelet been laid at his feet, the messenger would have been additionally welcome; but especially had the bearer of these tidings been able to say, as he showed the regalia, that he had first killed the defeated king, and then removed these tokens of royalty, he would have been intensely glad of the assurance of his enemy's death, and would have rewarded the slayer largely and liberally. And then, because he would have done so, with the instinct of a mean and inferior nature he proceeded to reckon that David would do precisely the same thing.

Now, whenever such judgments are formed, and on the same principle, it must be obvious that a considerable amount *of personal injustice* is perpetrated; and in reference, too, to that very point upon which a well-regulated mind will be most sensitive. To an upright man – to one who exercises himself to have a conscience void of offence towards God – character is a far more momentous consideration than thousands of silver and gold could ever be; and judgments formed on the principles of which this passage reminds us, do injustice to personal character. We feel, as we read the Amalekite's address, the injury to which David was thus subjected; and we think that it is not difficult to trace some symptoms that David felt, and keenly too, the injustice done to him in this respect. His very question, "How wast thou not afraid to stretch forth thine hand to destroy the Lord's anointed?" (*2 Samuel 1:14*), seems but another form of saying, "I would not for the world have done what you have done. You have mistaken me: you have judged of my feelings, of my principles, by your own. You have done me an injustice."

Nor is it to be wondered at that David should have felt the injustice acutely. For assuredly where, by the grace of God, a man has been taught the lesson of true self-respect – where he has been enabled, as the child of God, to hold that principle humbly, firmly, and for sanctified purposes – where the Spirit of God has produced moral elevation, and has stamped sin with its real character of debasement and dishonourableness – where these results have been brought about in the moral history of an individual, there is something very humiliating, something peculiarly distressing, because felt to be deeply degrading, in this very circumstance of having been so misunderstood and misjudged, as to have been supposed capable of finding gratification in acting out the principles which rule minds of another order, and of sympathising with the courses to which these principles conduct. There is scarcely a trial which is more hard to endure, or which pierces the heart with so deep a pang, than thus to find one's self standing, in the estimation of a man whose feelings and principles are low, on that same low platform which marks his own moral position, and side by side with himself. It may be said, indeed, that conscious integrity – the personal conviction of uprightness – ought to have a power to heal the pang, that it ought to be enough for a man to know that the judgment formed of him is wrong. But a more delicate perception will discover that it is this very circumstance which occasions the pang, which embitters the trial. It would be no trial but for this consciousness of personal integrity; and in employing this argument as a comfort to the child of God writhing beneath an injurious and unjust supposition, whether implied or expressed, the danger would be, that instead of mitigating the smart, you should only increase the anguish of the wound. The case to which we now refer requires delicate handling. Child of God, weeping and depressed, has thy spirit been broken and thy heart riven by such an injustice as that which has placed thy character on a low and unworthy level? has it been thy lot to be misjudged? has even a single mind regarded thee as sympathising with its own evil, with its own debasements, whether for the purpose of bringing an unjust accusation against thee before others, or of gaining private sanction to its own crafty purposes? Art thou looking for some relief beneath the trial? We will not blame thee for being too sensitive – in reference to character this can scarcely be: nor can we advise thee to meet the wrong judgment merely with thine own consciousness of integrity, for that might but aggravate the sorrow; but we would tell thee rather to yield to the trial meekly, and to find thy present solace and thine ultimate relief in the endeavour to ascertain the special ends which thy heavenly Father may have had in view in permitting the painful and humbling dispensation to befall thee, and in the prayerful effort to secure all the sanctified fruits of which such an affliction may, rightly improved, be productive. The understanding which has been spiritually enlightened, will be able to trace the salutary tendency of this peculiar form of trial. The very consciousness that the state of mind and feeling attributed to him is not that which is actually possessed by him, may lead – nay, must lead – the really upright man to a touching recognition of his own personal obligation to Almighty God for that bestowment of divine grace which has made all the difference. It may, it must, lead to the enquiry, "And how comes it to pass that the judgment thus formed of my character is erroneous? It might have been only too true. It might have fairly represented me. How comes it to pass, that I really do abhor the things which this man or that so readily supposes I could do as easily as himself? How comes it to pass, that I am conscious of no indulged sympathy with the course which he takes it for granted is as gratifying to me as to his own heart? Who hath made me to differ, and what have I which I have not received?" To such questionings the child of God can find but one reply – "By the grace of God I am what I am." He will freely acknowledge that if his life is free from the permitted power of those evil principles which are predominant in the conduct of others, it is not because those principles are less characteristic of his own heart by nature than of theirs, but because he has been graciously brought under another law, the law of the sanctifying Spirit. He will feel, too, that his only hope of continued integrity for the future, his only assurance that the sins which he now regards with abhorrence shall not gain the dominion over him, is to be found, not in any strength of his own, but in the continuance of that help from above, by which alone he already stands. So David felt: "By this I know that thou favourest me, because mine enemy doth not triumph over me. And as for me, thou upholdest me in mine integrity," (*Psalm 41:11, 12*).

Such recollections as these are indispensable to the maintenance of spiritual life. Especially do they supply a safeguard against spiritual pride, and afford a motive for perpetual dependence on "Him who is able to keep us from falling." Whatever else is forgotten, no child of God can afford to forget what he was till divine grace made the difference, and what he would become again if continued supplies of the same grace were not afforded him. Nothing so completely brings before him this spiritual portraiture of himself, as the wrong judgments which are formed of him, by those whose estimate of his character is founded on the lower principles and motives which are allowed to operate within their own unsanctified hearts, and on their own inability to comprehend the existence of anything higher – anything holier. The true solace, then, for the heart bleeding at the injustice perpetrated by a false and injurious estimate of character will be found in an intelligent view of those important ends which such a trial is peculiarly calculated to answer, and in yielding to the trial for the sake of the spiritual benefit which it is designed to promote. It may be hard to bear – it will be; yet it will be worthwhile to have had the spirit wounded by the injustice, and the heart depressed by the injury, if only the principles of gratitude to God, of humility, dependence, and caution, acquire power in the painful process; if only sin become more hateful – self become more completely laid in the dust – and God be more completely glorified. Ah! what a privilege it is – if, indeed, we have been made heirs of the heavenly kingdom – in those sorrows which come upon us from the wrong thoughts and unjust judgments of our fellow-men, to look away from man to God – to regard the things which befall us as occurring by His permission, though by man's instrumentality – to hear His fatherly voice inviting us, "Come, my people, enter thou into thy chambers, and shut thy doors about thee, and hide thyself for a little moment." (*Isaiah 26:20*). There, while we plead, "Remember, O Lord, what is come upon us: consider and behold our reproach," (*Lamentations 5:1*), we shall learn how true it is, that, "A bruised reed

He will not break, and the smoking flax He will not quench: He will bring forth judgment unto truth," (*Isaiah 42:3*); and we shall acquire from experience the assurance, that though "no chastening for the present seemeth to be joyous, but grievous: nevertheless afterward it yieldeth the peaceable fruit of righteousness unto them that are exercised thereby." (*Hebrews 12:11*).

So long as human nature is what it is – so long as men of corrupt minds want excuses for their sins, or sanction and encouragement in the commission of them – so long we must expect that they will find it convenient to form for themselves, and, if necessary, to present to others, a low and unjust estimate of the character of those whom divine grace has made the subjects of a better nature. But "the Lord taketh part with them that fear Him." He does so in this world – He will do it in the world to come; for there all tears will be wiped away, all reproach for ever removed; the whispers of those who watched for their halting will be hushed; the injustice of those who were ready to speak all manner of evil against them falsely, and the meanness of those who dared not speak openly, but who were ever ready to surmise and insinuate, will be forever past – the "well-done" and "welcome" of an omniscient God will be pronounced. The last clouds of earth shall be scattered; and those who have known their chilling and depressing influence "shall shine as the brightness of the firmament," and "as stars for ever and ever."

But let it not be thought by any that they can with impunity commit, under any circumstances, the injustice which has now been described. Apart from the injury which they inflict upon religious character by so representing it to themselves or to others, as that it shall be employed as a sanction for their own sins, or as an excuse for their wrong-doing, it must not be forgotten that, supposing the real character of a professor of religion were such as they represent it – supposing that beneath a profession of purity and love, in any instance, there really did exist a cherished impurity and an indulged malignity, from which they might gain encouragement in their plans, and from which they might secretly expect sanction, yet even this would not justify them in sinning. God looks at sinners in their individual capacity, and deals with them as such. Sin is felt by God to be a personal matter in reference to Himself, and nothing can justify its commission; no, not all the suspected hypocrisy, nor all the proved unfaithfulness of professors of religion, with all the imaginary sanction which the one might give, and all the real encouragement which the other would afford. If you could succeed in showing, with regard to all your professedly godly neighbours, that they were really just as fond of sin, as possessed of a low and worldly taste, and as prepared, when opportunity served, to gratify it, as this Amalekite thought David was ready to gratify a spirit of cold selfishness – this would not excuse your love of sin, your practice of what was morally inferior and unworthy. Your individual duty to be holy is independent of the question of your neighbour's conduct.

We know, indeed, that the formation of these wrong judgments of character constitutes a chosen method by which the great Enemy of souls seeks to entrap men to their own destruction. We believe that, in the case before us, the Amalekite acted out the thought of his own heart. But let us make a supposition of another kind – that there had been implicated in the matter someone who, though professedly the friend of that young man, was really and secretly his enemy, and whose desire it was to compass his ruin, to bring him to an untimely end. Let us suppose that this secret foe was perfectly well acquainted with David's real character and disposition – that he knew, especially, that he had repeatedly refused to take away Saul's life, and that therefore there was the highest reason to be sure that he would hold in abhorrence, and visit with extreme penalty, anyone who should stretch forth his hand against the Lord's anointed. Now, we ask, could that false friend have taken a more effectual step to accomplish his purpose of ruining that young man than to have suggested to him that, notwithstanding all that might be said or thought to the contrary, such was David's feeling about Saul, and such his anxiety by any means to ascend the throne, that if he would only go and persuade him that he had put an end to the king's existence, if he could only contrive to plunder the insignia of royalty, and take them to David as the confirmation of his account of the king's death, nothing would please the son of Jesse so much – that no scheme could be more promising for future advancement than this – that he would, assuredly, be made for life. How well that insidious device would have answered – how entirely that enemy in disguise would have succeeded – the actual death of the young man sufficiently indicates. Now, on such a supposition, we should want words to describe our horror of the cruelty and treachery, the deliberate murderousness of the heart which could have framed such a purpose for the young man's destruction, and carried it out so fatally. We should think it – call it – fiendish. Yet a scheme as fearfully insidious, as fully marked by deceit and cruelty, Satan is continually employing, with a malicious design to ruin souls, and especially the souls of the young. He belies and misrepresents religion in their view. He suggests that the high standard of a religious profession is a thing of imagination rather than of reality. He whispers stealthily that, notwithstanding the outward difference between the men whose lives are avowedly under a higher influence and the rest of mankind, it is not very difficult – for a consideration – to induce these very professors, either to act upon a lower principle themselves, or to give their sanction to those who adopt an inferior standard of religion and morals. He thus removes the checks and restraints which religious example and influence would exert in discouraging the young from evil. He does more; for, by the insinuation and imputation of real sympathy with sin on the part of professors, he gives direct encouragement to evil courses. Having thus, by acting out his character of "accuser of the brethren," produced an impression of personal religion as being hollow and valueless, the Enemy of souls next presents some well-adapted temptation – some well-arranged enticement – to secure present advantage by means which involve personal guilt and expose to heavy penalty. The scheme succeeds – the youth falls into the trap prepared for him – the criminal deed is done – the actual guilt is incurred – and then, the tempter's object being gained, conscience is allowed to speak, to make itself heard; and, amidst shame and misery, the discovery is made that the impressions about religion and religious professors which induced to the commission of sin, were wrong after all. Then the victim of the temptation wakes up to learn – what, indeed, he might have known before – what, indeed, he was under a responsibility to enquire into – what would have been very plain, if his own heart had not gone along with the tempter, and had not been blinded by the prospect of the pleasures of sin – that there is such a thing as religious principle; that it does produce a state of mind which holds sin in abhorrence; that it teaches men to press the enquiry for themselves, "How can I do this great wickedness, and sin against God?" and that it constrains them, in regard to others, to act a decided part, and to say, "I will set no wicked thing before mine eyes: I hate the work of them that turn aside; it shall not cleave to me ... He that worketh deceit shall not dwell within my house: he that telleth lies shall not tarry in my sight," (*Psalm 101:3, 7*). Well is it, when the timely discovery of the delusion which has been thus practised induces humility, and when the shame and confusion attendant on guilt issue in sincere repentance before God – in that repentance which hastens to rectify the error, and to act under the conviction that religion is a reality – that religious influence is a power of highest value, for the highest of purposes.

There is a fearful peril which the Scripture exposes to view, and to which nothing will so certainly conduct men, as this habit of misjudging the character of the people of God for the purpose of gaining sanction to their own sins. The transition is made from entertaining unjust and low thoughts of the people of God to forming unworthy and degrading views of God himself; and in the same way that a transgressor finds encouragement and sanction for personal sins in attributing to his fellow-creatures the same vicious motives which rule his own heart, so may he proceed a step further, and imagine that the Creator is altogether like himself. It would seem hardly credible, at first sight, that such an idea could ever find entrance in the human heart; but Omniscience records the fact as the object of its own discovery and censure – proving that there is no length to which the hardening influence of sin will not carry a man. Let the impressive words speak for themselves, in showing, at once, to what fearful extremes men may go in cherishing low and degrading thoughts of God – what awful moral consequences are the results of these thoughts – and what a terrible penalty comes in their train: "But unto the wicked God saith, What hast thou to do to declare my statutes, or that thou shouldest take my covenant in thy mouth? seeing thou hatest instruction, and castest my words behind thee. When thou sawest a thief, then thou consentedst with him, and hast been partaker with adulterers. Thou givest thy mouth to evil, and thy tongue frameth deceit. Thou sittest and speakest against thy brother; thou slanderest thine own mother's son. These things hast thou done, and I kept silence; *thou thoughtest that I was altogether such an one as thyself:* but I will reprove thee, and set them in order before thine eyes. Now, consider this, ye that forget God, lest I tear you in pieces, and there be none to deliver," (*Psalm 50:16-22*).

Chapter 13
The Elegy

"Tell it not in Gath, publish it not in the streets of Askelon; lest the daughters of the Philistines rejoice, lest the daughters of the uncircumcised triumph. Ye mountains of Gilboa, let there be no dew, neither let there be rain, upon you, nor fields of offerings: for there the shield of the mighty is vilely cast away, the shield of Saul, as though he had not been anointed with oil … Saul and Jonathan were lovely and pleasant in their lives, and in their death they were not divided: they were swifter than eagles, they were stronger than lions." (*2 Samuel 1:20, 21, 23*)

FROM the circumstances under which "David lamented with this lamentation over Saul and over Jonathan his son," we turn now to the elegy itself; and our first impressions must undoubtedly be those of interest in its highly poetical character and of admiration of its singular beauty and tenderness. The fall of the mighty – the dread of the Philistines' boast – the wish that henceforth a barren dreariness might rest upon Gilboa, commemorative of the desolation of Israel and of the defeat of their king – the tribute to the courage of Jonathan and to the bravery of Saul – the exploits of the one with his sword, and of the other with his bow – the memory of those early days when the spirit of that father, not yet soured by the indulgence of evil passions, was wont to send forth its strong affections towards the lovely Jonathan, and to receive back a full measure of filial love – the relieving thought that in the circumstances of their death there was a conformity to the best period of their lives, that they were together when they died – the kindly notice of that measure of outward prosperity which at times had attended the reign of Saul – and then the distress, the heart-breaking distress, as the full consciousness pressed upon David's spirit that the link which had bound his own soul to Jonathan had been snapped asunder on the field of blood – all these crowd upon our minds as we read the touching lines, and produce emotions of the strongest sympathy with the weeping warrior as he pours forth the sorrows of his soul. The sacred historian informs us that this lamentation, under the title of "The Bow," found a permanent place, among other compositions relating to the history of Israel, in the book of Jasher; and from thence, when the inspired narrative was compiled, it was transferred to its present position in the pages of holy writ. We say, "under the title of 'The Bow,'" for there is no authority for the insertion of the words "the use of" in our version of *2 Samuel 1:18*. The history gives us no idea that the use of the bow was so rare in the tribe of Judah that it was necessary to give them instructions in this kind of warfare; and the passage, rightly rendered, reads thus – "Also he bade them teach the children of Judah the Bow." That the name, "The Bow," should have been given to this funeral-song was only in accordance with a custom of which we meet with many instances in titles affixed to the compositions preserved to us in the *Book of Psalms*; and the reason of the selection of this title was, in all probability, either the circumstance that it was by the use of the bow the Philistines did such terrible execution on that fatal day at Gilboa, or else the choice of this name for the song of mourning might have arisen from the recollection of the use which Jonathan made of his own bow on that memorable occasion when the flight of the arrow indicated to David, in concealment, the presence of his friend, and the ill tidings of which he was the bearer; and when, before they separated, they made a covenant with each other, "and they kissed one another, and wept one with another, until David exceeded." (*1 Samuel 20:41*).

But amidst all these emotions of interest and admiration which are called up by the perusal of this exquisite composition, we cannot altogether dismiss from our minds a consciousness of at least an apparent discrepancy, as far as Saul is concerned, between the tone in which David expresses himself in reference to him, and the general impression which we have of Saul's character, founded on the actual facts of his history. In the minds of those whose habit it is not to take everything for granted, and who are accustomed to enquire into the reasons of things, the question will arise, "Was this really the kind of elegy which we should have expected that a good man like David would have pronounced over such an one as Saul? If there be historic truthfulness in the view which the preceding chapters give of the life and conduct of the first king of Israel, then is not the language of this dirge, commemorative of his death, somewhat inconsistent with the representations given of his life? Is there not the putting forth of only a partial, a very partial, view of Saul? Would it not have been better if less had been said of him? Have not many men far superior to Saul, men whose holiness the Scriptures record, received a far less favourable notice when they have gone out of the world?"

Now, we conceive that such questionings are highly reasonable, and are, therefore, by no means to be discouraged. They admit, too, we believe, of satisfactory solution; and the process by which we arrive at this solution is itself inviting, because it affords the opportunity of bestowing a thought or two on some other points connected with an intelligent view of the Holy Scriptures.

We are far from assigning the peculiar complexion of this elegy to that mere commonplace thing which goes by the name, though most wrongfully, of charity; but which should rather be character-ised as perilous unfaithfulness to God, to the interests of religion, and to the safety of men's souls – a charity which is, however, very popular with a certain class of persons who are ever ready to throw its mantle over the defects of others, provided that they can man-age, at the same time, to effect concealment beneath its folds for some indulged sins of their own. Nor can we perceive in this com-position the utterance of a spirit of flattery, which, to answer an end, can speak good things of a bad man with cool effrontery, and with perfect consciousness of the falsehood which the lips are utter-ing. There was no end to be answered here which would serve as a temptation; and how little sympathy there was in David's mind with such a practice, we may gather from those repeated expressions of abhorrence in regard to it which meet us in his writings. Describing the conduct of the wicked, he says, "There is no faithfulness in their mouth; they flatter with their tongue," (*Psalm 5:9*); and in another instance, "They speak vanity every one with his neighbour: with flattering lips and with a double heart do they speak. The Lord shall cut off all flattering lips," (*Psalm 12:2, 3*). Still less do we discover in these words of David nothing more than a tribute to the claims which death is allowed to put forth for a respectful mention of the departed. We cannot regard it as a mere exemplification of the doctrine, good enough within certain limits, that when a man is dead his failings are not to be made the subject of remark – a doctrine which, however, becomes mischievous, when it allows survivors to trifle with the best interests of society – either by being silent in cases where truth and faithfulness demand that, by allusion to the dead, appropriate and solemn caution should be conveyed to the living, or by dishonestly pronouncing such eulogies on the departed as are calculated to produce altogether a false impression of their personal character and conduct. The practices we condemn are, alas! too common. There are cases, like that of Saul, in which we are not surprised when conscious guilt and its attendant misery have led men to lay violent hands on themselves. Aware of their real character, the intelligence which startles us is – not that they are dead, nor that they died as suicides – but we are startled by the discovery all at once made of excellences which were never heard of till they were gone, and of unimpeachable moral rectitude to which they certainly did not themselves pretend while they were living. But to none of these causes can David's elegy be referred.

I. In accounting for the peculiar tone of this funeral-song, in its allusion to Saul – so apparently at variance as it is, in some respects, with the character and conduct of the deceased king, and involving the discrepancy even of ascribing what was "lovely and beautiful" to one who leaves a most unlovely impression upon the mind – the history seems to justify us in regarding the elegy itself as the testimony which David desired to bear to the completeness with which he forgave Saul every injury which he had inflicted on him – every wrong which he had ever attempted to do him. It is his public attestation to the utter absence of any, even the least, feelings of personal resentment. He speaks as though he had entirely forgotten all past unkindnesses; as though, by some extraordinary process, they had been completely obliterated from the tablet of his memory. As far as personal offence had been felt, all was utterly removed. He could contemplate various relationships which subsisted between the departed king and himself, and overlook the fact that in their progress, from the moment when they commenced till the time at which death put an end to them, Saul had ever offered him an insult, or occasioned him a pang.

There is nowhere to be found in Scripture a more striking and complete exemplification of human forgiveness. There is nowhere an instance which so entirely reminds us of the way in which divine forgiveness manifests itself. In indicating to us the nature and extent of that pardon which God is ready to bestow on those who seek it, the Scriptures reveal to us the Most High thus expressing Himself: *"I have blotted out, as a thick cloud, thy transgressions, and, as a cloud, thy sins,"* (*Isaiah 44:22*). *"I will forgive their iniquity, and I will remember their sin no more,"* (*Jeremiah 31:34*). "In those days, and in that time, *the iniquity* of Israel shall *be sought for,* and there *shall be none;* and the *sins* of Judah, and *they shall not be found:* for I will *pardon* them whom I reserve," (*Jeremiah 50:20*). These were the views, too, of divine forgiveness which were cherished by the servants of God. Thus we find the prophet Isaiah inviting sinners to return to God; and using, as his argument, the extent of His forgiving grace, "For He will *abundantly* pardon," (*Isaiah 55:7*). It was this completeness of the removal of offence which gladdened the good king Hezekiah, when he said, "Thou hast in love to my soul delivered it from the pit of corruption: for thou *hast cast all my sins behind thy back,"* (*Isaiah 38:17*); and it was under the deep and overwhelming impression of the same view of the entireness with which God exercises pardoning love, that the prophet Micah exclaimed, "Who is a God like unto thee, that pardoneth iniquity, and *passeth by the transgression* of the remnant of His heritage? He retaineth not His anger for ever, because He delighteth in mercy. He will turn again, He will have compassion upon us; He will subdue our iniquities; and *thou wilt cast all their sins into the depths of the sea,"* (*Micah 7:18, 19*). Receiving, then, these descriptions of the entireness and thoroughness with which God acts when He forgives sin, the utter absence of any feeling of resentment, the never allowing it to become the occasion of condemnation – do we not discover the traces of an unusually close imitation of the divine character and procedure in the manner in which David here refers to Saul? Do we not see at work the heart of one who has completely *"blotted out"* the impression of the cruel persecution which Saul had carried on against him – who had "*cast behind his back*" all personal offence – who had no desire "*to remember any more*" one of the many occasions on which his own spirit had been riven by the ill-treatment and jealousy of him for whom he had repeatedly hazarded his own life? We may accept it as helping to illustrate that view which the Scriptures give of the purpose and the power of divine grace, when they speak of the people of God becoming as "partakers of the divine nature," and as being "renewed after the image of Him that created them." In regard to one aspect of moral character, and that one the manifestation of which involves a difficult encounter with, and a great victory over predominant self, David's example serves to show what measures of resemblance to God – of "bearing the image of the heavenly" – may be, by divine grace, attained by man. It serves to show how we may be "imitators of God;" how we may "walk worthy of the Lord, unto all pleasing." There is no one duty which is enforced upon us with more decisive clearness, and with more frequent repetition, than that of forgiving, of abstaining from personal resentment in cases where injury has been inflicted; and inasmuch as, with the practice of these requirements, God associates His own forgiveness as our rule and principle of guidance, it must be advantageous to study a case such as that now before us. It not only exhibits the spirit which we are bound to manifest, but does this in such a form as that we cannot fail, while contemplating the conduct of the creature, to trace in it the close imitation – by the aid of divine grace – of the Creator; and, when admiring the manner in which David forgave, to see reflected in it, with peculiar force and beauty, the distinctive features which characterise the dealings of God, in the same direction.

II. While the entireness with which David had forgiven Saul is testified in the absence from this death-song of any reference to the painfulness of the past – an absence so complete that, had we not known the reverse from the history, we might have imagined that the two men had been bosom friends, the elder and the younger living on terms of the most uninterrupted mutual kindness – yet this circumstance, on which we have been dwelling, may not of itself fully account for another feature of the elegy. There is not only the absence of condemnatory allusion, but there is the presence of a considerable amount of matter of a positively and uniformly commendatory character. Now, it is quite certain that David felt that every word which he uttered would be borne out by fact – that he knew it would be accepted as being quite capable of proof; or else he would not have ventured on the publication of this dirge, and most assuredly he would not have required that it should have been taught while the circumstances of Saul's life were still fresh in the memory of men. And yet, where is the thoughtful reader who is not prepared to confess that the impression which David's language is naturally calculated to make upon the mind is not exactly the impression which we receive from the perusal of Saul's history, looked at as a whole?

In following up the enquiry suggested by this discrepancy, we must remember that it happens with descriptions of character, as it does with delineations of outward nature – *they are taken from particular points of view,* and must, of course, vary greatly, and differ from each other according to the standpoint selected for making the observation or forming the sketch. In order to identify with the actual scenery a representation by the pencil of some inviting landscape, or of any particular objects which give it interest, we must take the trouble to find out the precise spot at which the artist stood, and forth from which he looked abroad when he sketched the picture; we must go and stand there ourselves, and if we will only do this, we shall be in a condition to judge of the truthfulness of the representation, and it may be that we shall find ourselves prepared to admit most fully the correctness of some lines and features in the picture, about the accuracy of which we may have previously entertained grave doubts. Thus, too, in estimating the truthfulness of sketches of individual character, we are not at liberty to take up our position exactly where we like; the only fair way of forming a judgment of the portraiture, is to find out the standpoint at which the author of the sketch fixed himself, and, adopting it as our own, we must, from that position, make our observation. Any other course would obviously be unjust. We should conceive it very unreasonable, if a man – standing on the *North* terrace of that magnificent structure, the stately Castle of our beloved Queen, and holding in his hand a view of the surrounding park and the distant scenery, taken from the *East* terrace – were to complain that the artist had only given a very partial view of the royal estate. We should listen, probably, with increasing impatience while this stranger went on to say, that in what he had attempted the artist had made mistakes, for some objects were not depicted in the sketch which could, nevertheless, be distinctly seen, and which, therefore, ought to have been noticed; while others were most unaccountably introduced, which certainly were not visible to him. We should wait, perhaps, till he declared, that though there was foliage in the picture, yet the lines of far-spreading trees which rose before him stood altogether in a different direction from those which the artist had employed his pencil to sketch; and then we should, with what composure we could command, reply, "It is not the picture which is wrong. You are at fault yourself. For in the first place, that sketch which you hold in your hand does not profess to include more than the prospect from one side of the edifice; it is not intended, by any means, to give the whole of those surrounding views of nature's loveliness and splendour which, from its noble heights, that regal palace commands. It is the sketch of only a portion of the scenery, and that portion itself not that which corresponds to the spot at which you are now standing. But have the goodness to advance a little, and you will find yourself on the East terrace, and then and there, if you will compare the view which meets your eye with that which is delineated in the sketch which you hold in your hand, you will see that there is truthfulness in the artist's effort, after all: he has drawn it just *as it appears from that spot.*"

An illustration so homely as that which we have now selected is all that is required for judging rightly of the case before us. The true key to the elegy which David here pronounced is the point of view from which he looked at Saul – the position, in relation to the departed monarch, which he occupied at the moment. He simply noted down the features of character and aspects of conduct which met his eye where he stood; and if we will go and stand side by side with him, looking as he looked, and feeling as he felt, we shall at once acknowledge the accuracy of his portraiture. There are some circumstances which are peculiarly favourable for forming a full and accurate estimate of an individual; there are others, however, which only permit us to take a limited view at best, and looking from the midst of these, the eye most generally allows itself to be engrossed with one or two characteristic features, which come very near ourselves, and which appear, for that very reason, separated in a measure from all the rest.

At such a point David now stood. He sketched Saul just as he could see him from that spot; and as he drew the portrait for a special purpose, the Author of the Bible laid hold of it – retained it – and gave it a place among the many portraits which meet the eye of the reader of Scripture, when he opens its pages for a purpose, than which none can be more important – that of studying character.

Our own experience will, in all probability, conduct us easily and directly to the precise point from which this sketch of Saul was taken. We have only to ask ourselves, When is it that we feel ourselves shut up to one aspect of an individual's character, and that one the most favourable? when is it that we busy ourselves in recollecting all that was pleasant in his intercourse with us, and calling up everything that was creditable in the eyes of others? and when is it that there is the greatest corresponding facility in not remembering anything which was the reverse of either pleasant or creditable? Is it not when we find, for the first time, that instead of having to deal with our fellow-creature as among the living, we have to think of him as numbered with the dead? when our hearts are subdued by the first, and perhaps the sudden, intelligence of his departure? Ah! have you never seen how that while the first gush of tears was scarcely spent, the tongue of the bereaved parent would betake itself to describe some excellences of her departed son? and although his character might have been marked by something else than excellences, and something, alas! the opposite of them too; and although whatever features of interest attached to his conduct, it was long – long ago – since he manifested any of them; yet you hear nothing at all of the painful part now, and you might suppose – from the tone of that simple and unlaboured dirge which the lips of the wailing mother are pronouncing – that her child had never caused her a tear, had never committed a fault! Ah! have you not felt it – have you not done it, when – having heard of the death of one who had been in earlier days your friend, and whom you never could forget, though circumstances reflecting discredit on himself had constrained you long ago to withdraw from him – you could not but remember that you had loved him, though you had been forced to blame him, and to refuse to continue that outward manifestation of friendship which would have been justly construed into a sanction of his evil courses. Yet no sooner did the intelligence reach you that he was dead, no sooner did you feel that this was really true, than there rose before you the memory of those days when you and he "took sweet counsel together," and when as yet the evil spirit had not acquired the power over him, which marred the character of your friend, and destroyed your own peace and comfort. And as you called up the scenes and circumstances of former times, the aspect was so lovely, and the view so pleasant, that memory took its pencil, and sketched it at the moment, and in that picture no offence which he ever committed against you has a place, no injury he ever inflicted upon you is marked down; nor would it be known, from that portraiture of his life and character, that he had ever grieved you at all. No! you could not have found it in your heart to have said a single word, or to have expressed a single thought, which would have told how ill he had treated you. It is true, that the manner in which you referred to the departed might have sounded strangely in the ears of others, yet you had only taken the view which grief would naturally receive – the grief of a bereaved and sorrowing heart – when you heard that the friend of your early days was no more.

And now, if, under the influence of these recollections, we will study the case before us – strange as it may seem that a man like Saul was lamented by David in such an elegy as this, all painful idea of discrepancy will be removed. He did what was simply natural for him to do. He stood at that point, mentally, from which he could catch sight just of those features of Saul's history and character which he has here marked down. If, in imagination, we stand by his side, and look in the same direction, we shall be struck with the truthfulness of the portraiture; we shall see, faithfully noted, those very aspects under which David had been wont, in other days, to contemplate the man who was at once his sovereign and his friend, but who stood out prominently to view as the father of the beloved Jonathan, and was seen to greater advantage from this circumstance. We shall find ourselves brought back to the time when Saul and Jonathan – father and son – were always seen together, and in such loving and pleasant intercourse as that they rather appeared like two brothers – the elder with the younger – confiding in each other's affection, and living for each other's welfare. We shall gain the vision of those days when, loved by both, David sat in the kingly residence – the intimate friend of Jonathan, the indispensable companion of Saul; and then there will come, in connection with such a retrospect, the remembrance of

Jonathan's courage, and of his father's early exploits – a remembrance which will make the heart bleed to think of the two falling together on the field of battle, and closing their earthly existence amid the same scenes of defeat and slaughter. And for the moment we shall forget that ever Saul needed to be held back by a popular demonstration from putting Jonathan to death; or that on repeated occasions and in various forms he had, with fearful determination and with extraordinary malevolence, sought to take away the life of David. Standing where David did, these things did not come within the range of his vision – they formed no part of the view which opened up before his eyes. That view contained only what was creditable in Saul's life, and pleasant in David's recollection. It was no part of his intention to produce a history of the first king of Israel; but simply to pour forth the strong feelings of his heart, when he heard that Saul was no more, and that his best-beloved Jonathan was lying dead with his father on the same field of blood.

Such we may deem to be the reason fairly assignable for the peculiar character of this lamentation which David pronounced over Saul; and, thus regarded, its introduction into the sacred volume answers a most important purpose. It presents us with that which we must admit to be a beautiful specimen of genuine nature. It makes us feel, taking this as a sample of Scripture history, that the records of individuals which are furnished us in the Bible are *bona fide* what they profess to be; that they are authentic biographies; and that in them we have not to do with delineations unreal, far-fetched, and got up for an occasion. We gain thus a comfortable conviction of the truthfulness of the volume – of the reliable character of its contents.

Nor is this all. In such manifestations of natural feeling as we discover in this and other passages of the same order, there is much that is encouraging, in a practical point of view. We find our spirits brought into contact with men "of like passions" with ourselves. In David, as he uttered this elegy, we see a man who could weep, just as we weep; who could break down with the pressure of sudden bereavement, just as we break down; who, under the influence of sorrows, looked at men and things just as, under the same influence, we look at them. He does not stand apart from us as a being of higher nature, whose superiority should awe us, and keep us at a discouraging distance; but he comes near to us, and wins our interested attention.

We can feel at home with him; we can read his heart as that of a fellow-creature; we can understand him as a man. Considering the large space which David occupies on the page of Scripture, as an example of what is strong in holy confidence and exalted in piety towards God and communion with Him, it is impossible to attach too much momentousness to the point to which we are referring. We can readily conceive the case of some earnest but humble religious enquirer, struck with the peculiar characteristics of David's devotion on some occasions – affected by the utterance which he employs, by the spirit which he breathes – we can conceive such an one longing to appropriate to his own use some of those holy, happy sentences which are preserved in the sacred volume, as the memorials of the manner in which he had fellowship with the Most High, but yet entertaining a vague sort of feeling that there might have been something very peculiar in David's character, which made him different from ordinary men – that this undefined superiority raised him above the usual tone of human feelings and the wonted limits of human views, and placed him therefore at a great advantage in reference to the maintenance of confidence in God in trial, and of communion with Him amid the accustomed engagements of life. It is easy to calculate the discouraging effects of such a conception – "Would that I could attain to the same high degree of confidence as that which David felt when he cried out, 'The Lord is my light and my salvation; whom shall I fear? the Lord is the strength of my life; of whom shall I be afraid?' Would that I could rejoice as David rejoiced when he wrote, 'Who is God save the Lord? or who is a rock save our God? It is God that girdeth me with strength, and maketh my way perfect. He maketh my feet like hinds' feet, and setteth me upon my high places.' Would that I could say, as David said, 'My heart is fixed, O God, my heart is fixed. I will sing and give praise. Awake up, my glory; awake psaltery and harp: I myself will awake early.' But I feel that there is such a difference between David and myself, that it is useless to expect that I should be or do in religion what he was and what he did. He was not constituted as I am. He was far superior in the natural tone of his feelings and direction of his thoughts; and I cannot hope to reach the measure of his personal religion – of his heart-felt converse with God." Now, in reply to all such thoughts, we can at once pronounce that they are erroneous – that they are proved to be so by many portions of David's history – and by none more so than by the utterance of this funeral-song. He stands on the level of a common humanity with every reader of the narrative. It is human nature which we recognise at work – a nature like our own. It is a man shedding tears as we shed them, and doing exactly the same things as, we are disposed to think, we should have done under the same circumstances. And we argue from this point, and argue hopefully. We say to the discouraged spirit, "You see that David and you are alike as regards human nature. Divine grace has the same material on which to work in your case as in his, the same views of things in general, the same emotions under particular dispensations – then why should not divine grace do for you what it did for him? meeting you on the same level as that at which it met him, why should it not conduct you to the same point to which it elevated him? If, in David's case, the start, so to speak, in holy attainments had been made by him from a nature which was not in every respect like your own, from a nature which had not the same feelings, and took not the same views – then, indeed, you might fear that you, starting from a less advanced position, might never reach the point which he gained; and so his example might be a perpetual discouragement. Now you cannot with fairness receive this impression when you look at David as, at this point of history, he appears before you – a man in distress of mind giving way to the tears of humanity, and affording proof that the occurrences of time affected him as they affect you." This principle is applicable to the many histories of the people of God which meet us in the Bible; and the more thoroughly it is felt, the more will the reflecting mind gain motives for encouragement in the pursuit of holiness and peace, and the more will it find reasons for thankfulness to that God who, in constructing a book for our guidance, embodied so large an amount of instruction in the actual history of men "of like passions" with ourselves.

Reverting from the elegy, however, to the man over whom it was pronounced, it is important that we should bear in mind that our destiny in the next world will be decided, not by the estimate which survivors may, under any circumstances, form of our character and conduct, but by the view which the eye of Omniscience has taken of us, from the beginning to the termination of our earthly existence. It will not be the record of our life – written by the hand of human friendship, and exhibiting but a partial view of what we were and what we did – which will meet us at God's tribunal, but the pages of the book of God's remembrance will be opened then, presenting the most exact transcript of each portion of our existence, however minute. The account to which every man will be summoned will comprehend "the things done in his body" in the whole course of life.

The elegy which friendship has composed, and grief has pronounced, will not follow the spirit of the departed into the next world, to effect an alteration in its condition, if the awful sentence should have gone forth from the lips of that immutably just Being who proceeds upon the whole conduct of a man, and who will not accept the outward excellences which have met the eye of his fellow-creatures on some occasions, as a set-off against the disobedience of the heart towards Himself, and the rejection by the spirit of His kind entreaties and merciful invitations to holiness and peace. How affecting is the contrast which, alas! there is too much reason to fear would sometimes be presented between what survivors are doing and saying in reference to individuals who have left the world, and the actual condition of the souls of those individuals, if for a moment we could be admitted to make ourselves certainly acquainted with it. How many we would find "lifting up his eyes in hell, being in torment," as having lived "without God in the world," whose manly form the artist's chisel has preserved from being forgotten, and whose earthly virtues are graven on the marble beneath. Ah! could the spectators of that monument, which tells of deeds of valour done and of glory earned, see the spectacle in the next world which corresponds to the "storied urn or animated bust" before which he stands – could he track the spirit which, covered with shame and confusion, lives now and will forever live to attest the truth of God's Word – "Be not deceived; God is not mocked: for whatsoever a man soweth, that shall he also reap. For he that soweth to his flesh shall of the flesh reap corruption," (*Galatians 6:7, 8*), – how overwhelming would be the impression of the awful discrepancy between the views of man and the decisions of God! how deep our conviction of the possibility that an individual may stand well in the memory of his fellow-creatures, while in another world he may be forever reaping the bitter consequences of not having his "heart right with God!"

Ah! could some listener to that mention of the departed, from which grief, in its natural utterance, is excluding all remembrance of transgressions which were known, and sins which in life could not be concealed – could some such listener compare what human lips are breathing in tones of sorrow and of entire forgiveness, with the words which the divine Judge is uttering and enforcing – how resistlessly would the conviction be forced upon the hearer's heart, that a man's sins may be forgiven by his fellow-creatures in this world, and yet that they may not be forgiven by God in the next! This is an awful truth; but it is one which is too much and too fatally overlooked. *Our fellow-creatures may forgive us, but we may yet go into eternity unpardoned by God.* And this, not because man is kinder to his fellow than God is to His creatures. No! but because of the unwillingness of sinful man to seek pardon in that way in which alone God dispenses it, and in which, while He passes by transgression, His law is honoured, His truth is maintained, and the respect due to His moral government is ensured. In the atonement effected by the Son of God, to which all sacrifice pointed, and which was made known from the earliest time with sufficient clarity to meet the case of sinful men, that way of forgiveness is discovered – God, for Christ's sake, forgives men their trespasses. To this propitiation all are invited, with the assurance that none who come in faith and repentance shall be rejected. If, therefore, men die unforgiven by God, it is not because the divine way of pardon is difficult and inaccessible, but because the offer being graciously made, His mercy has been refused through ingratitude, or its advantages lost through procrastination.

Such reflections as these will not have suggested themselves to us in vain, if we are led by them to place above every other consideration the necessity of immediately seeking and satisfactorily attaining the remission of our sins by God Himself, through a believing and repenting application to Jesus Christ, the sinner's Surety – the only Mediator between God and man. We cannot, indeed, without incurring additional guilt, neglect the duty of seeking the forgiveness of our fellow-creatures, when we have given them pain; but never let us allow reconciliation with men and re-instatement in their kind thoughts, to be a substitute for peace with God – for that reconciliation, the sense of which is the strongest motive for holy obedience – that reconciliation which must be attained by us before we die or not at all. The

lips of sorrowing friends may make no record of our sad wander-
ings in heart and life, but God may not have forgotten nor forgiven
them. Our elegy may be written with all the touching tenderness of
friendship, and all the inspiration of true poetic feeling; and yet our
names may not be inscribed in "the Lamb's Book of Life." In the same
memorial we may be mentioned together with "the blessed who die
in the Lord;" but beyond the grave they may be where we shall never
join them: and from these "pious dead" it may be ours to be enduring
a hopeless separation, while, as the passer-by glances down the tablet,
and reads the records of mortality, his lips are pronouncing of us and
of them, "In their deaths they were not divided."

— THE END —

Made in United States
North Haven, CT
11 August 2022

22589322R00102